GRADE 3

Week-by-Week Homework:
Reading Comprehension

MARY ROSE
with contributing authors
Margaret S. Gentile and Ann Sullivan Sheldon

NEW YORK ● TORONTO ● LONDON ● AUCKLAND ● SYDNEY
MEXICO CITY ● NEW DELHI ● HONG KONG ● BUENOS AIRES

Acknowledgments: My special thanks to the people at Scholastic Teaching Resources who made this series of books possible, especially Virginia Dooley, Mela Ottaiano, and Sarah Glasscock

Dedication: To Tom Rose, my ever patient, loving, and helpful husband

Photos © : 19: Hulton Archive/Getty Images; 34 top: Cloud7Days/iStockphoto; 34 center: loops7/iStockphoto; 34 bottom: anna1311/iStockphoto; 47: Rita Kochmarjova/Shutterstock, Inc.; 49: Blend Images/Shutterstock, Inc.; 52: Tipp Howell/Getty Images; 54: Michael Caulfield/AP Images; 56: Michael Regan/Getty Images; 59: Bettmann/Corbis Images; 61: Topical Press Agency/Getty Images; 63: The Washington Post/Getty Images; 66: Photo Researchers/Getty Images; 68: Anna Kucherova/Shutterstock, Inc.; 71 top: Matej Divizna/Getty Images; 71 bottom: Education Images/Getty Images; 73: Kathy Kay/Shutterstock, Inc.; 75: compassandcamera/iStockphoto; 80: Andrew Watson/Getty Images; 83: cbpix/iStockphoto; 85 top left: SolStock/iStockphoto; 85 top right: Piepereit/iStockphoto; 85 bottom left: KidStock/Getty Images; 85 bottom right: Ty Allison/Getty Images; 88 top: duncan1890/iStockphoto; 88 bottom: De Agostini Picture Library/Getty Images; 90: London Stereoscopic Company/Getty Images; 93: Wolfgang Kaehler/Getty Images.

Text credits: "Super Hound," p. 17; "The Dragon and the Stone," p. 28 by Margaret S. Gentile; "Gabby's Gold," p. 56; "Pelican Pete," p. 73; "Lady Liberty," p. 75; "Do Your Shoes Talk?," p. 88; "Can You Spot the Leopard?," p. 93 by Ann Sullivan Sheldon.

Cover design: Tannaz Fassihi
Cover illustration: Patrick George
Interior design: Melinda Belter
Interior illustrations: Kelly Kennedy; Rose Mary Berlin (pp. 28, 43, 44); George Ulrich (p. 37); Lynn Stevens Massey (p. 78)
Editor: Sarah Glasscock
Copy editor: Carol Ghiglieri

Contents

LITERARY TEXT ASSIGNMENTS

Key Ideas and Details

RL.3.1 Ask and answer questions to demonstrate understanding of a text, referring explicitly to the text as the basis for the answers.

RL.3.2 Recount stories, including fables, folktales, and myths from diverse cultures; determine the central message, lesson, or moral and explain how it is conveyed through key details in the text.

RL.3.3 Describe characters in a story (e.g., their traits, motivations, or feelings) and explain how their actions contribute to the sequence of events.

Craft and Structure

RL.3.4 Determine the meaning of words and phrases as they are used in a text, distinguishing literal from nonliteral language.

RL.3.5 Refer to parts of stories, dramas, and poems when writing or speaking about a text, using terms such as chapter, scene, and stanza; describe how each successive part builds on earlier sections.

RL.3.6 Distinguish their own point of view from that of the narrator or those of the characters.

Integration of Knowledge and Ideas

RL.3.7 Explain how specific aspects of a text's illustrations contribute to what is conveyed by the words in a story (e.g., create mood, emphasize aspects of a character or setting).

(RL.3.8 not applicable to literature)

RL.3.9 Compare and contrast the themes, settings, and plots of stories written by the same author about the same or similar characters (e.g., in books from a series).

INFORMATIONAL TEXT ASSIGNMENTS

Key Ideas and Details

RI.3.1 Ask and answer questions to demonstrate understanding of a text, referring explicitly to the text as the basis for the answers.

Introduction

A Note From the Author

Homework can be a valuable link between what you do in the classroom and the parents you serve, but many parents say they struggle to make the most of homework time. According to a 2014 survey conducted by the National Center for Families Learning (NCFL), 60 percent of parents struggle to help with their children's homework assignments (NCFL, 2014). The biggest challenges to helping their children with homework were time and a lack of understanding about the subject.

Your efforts in planning and assigning homework can make a significant impact in empowering parents to be teaching partners. The simple process used in this series of week-by-week assignments establishes an effective routine that can enrich a family's experience with reading. Just imagine the cumulative effect this type of support would have on a child who received it from grades 1 to 6; the weekly minutes add up to hours of added involvement and growth in reading skills. And it can all happen in two chairs at the kitchen table or on the living room couch. As an educator, you have the unique opportunity to invite both students and parents to learn and grow.

I always welcome your feedback at marycrose@mac.com.

Mary Rose

How to Use This Book

This book has been carefully written to be a *homework* book—a link between you and your students' families to bridge the gap between school and home. The passages in this book are correlated to the Common Core State Standards (CCSS). The passages and sets of questions will provide children with weekly practice in a particular reading skill correlated to the CCSS. The passages and questions might be slightly easier than those you are presenting in your classroom, but that is intentional. We want children to experience success as they practice the skills they've learned.

The book is divided into two parts: literary texts and informational texts. I suggest you begin with the easiest passages in the literary text section. This will provide children with read-aloud practice and teach them how to answer questions

Week-by-Week Homework: Reading Comprehension (Grade 3)
© Mary Rose, Scholastic Inc.

relating to the text. Most standards have more than one passage. This allows you to teach a particular lesson to your whole class, and then assign different homework lessons based on the reading ability of individual children. It also enables you to return to skills you have already taught and review them later in the school year, and to assign more difficult pages as children's reading ability progresses. Here's a brief overview of the structure of an assignment:

The **WELCOME LETTER** to families introduces the concept behind this type of homework. At the beginning of the school year, make a copy of the letter on pages 13–14 for each child to take home. This letter also includes suggestions about how families can help their children improve their reading skills.

Each assignment begins with a **TEACHER TALK** page. More information on the standard appears here, along with suggestions and tips for applying it.

The **FAMILY LETTER WITH QUESTIONS** page begins with a short note about the passage that gives directions and suggestions about how families can help their children before, during, and after reading. Following the note is a series of questions to complete after reading the passage. At the back of the book is an answer key for the questions. The child and a family member should sign the bottom of the page to indicate they completed the assignment together. The child will return this page to you for grading. Additional information on the page identifies the standard, and there is space to write the date on which the assignment is due.

The **READ-ALOUD** page contains a literary or informational passage for children to read aloud to a family member.

Note that Standard 10 is not addressed in a particular assignment, but doing these homework assignments will certainly help children work toward the goal of that standard—reading grade-level texts independently by the end of the year.

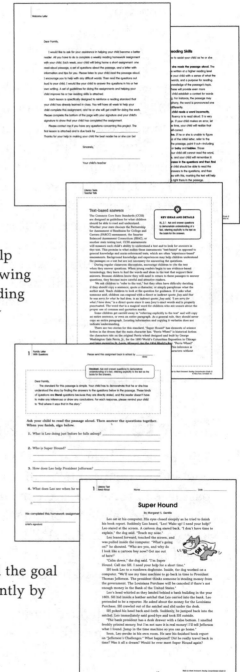

Week-by-Week Homework: Reading Comprehension (Grade 3)
© Mary Rose, Scholastic Inc.

Cycling through an assignment

Each week, select one read-aloud passage to assign for reading homework. I suggest the following procedure:

Assign a homework assignment on Monday and ask for it to be returned by Friday. On the following Monday, call small groups together to discuss the work. Review the skill, focusing on words and questions that presented difficulty. If there is a natural connection between the assignment and the next one, share it with children. Then, hand out the new assignment. Take a few moments to discuss the topic of the passage, pointing out difficult words and reviewing the standard. Depending on children's skill level, you might even have them read the passage in small groups before sending the assignment home.

Grading and monitoring homework assignments

The easiest way to grade these assignments is to give whole credit, half credit, or no credit. This simplified grading system is designed to meet the broad range of assistance that families provide to their children. Some family members assist by writing down the answers for the child; others will allow the child to write his or her own answers; and still others will encourage a child to work until every letter in the answer is correct. Some children can complete their homework with no assistance at all; others need a bit of gentle assistance. Be sure to emphasize this point when you meet with families for conferences. Help each family establish reasonable expectations related to their child's abilities. Revisit this issue as the school year progresses, emphasizing that the goal is for families to gradually offer less assistance as children gain confidence and skills in reading.

When you communicate with a family, ask them how long it's taking their child to complete a homework assignment. If it takes longer than 20 minutes, the passages are too difficult. If it takes less than 5 minutes, they are too easy. Differentiate the assignments for children by assigning easier or more difficult passages in this book. If the lessons are still too easy, you may want to use assignments from the grade 4 book in this series.

Using a passage with more than one standard

Almost any passage in this book can be correlated to several standards. Most passages can be used for a lesson on main idea, retelling, or finding unfamiliar vocabulary words. However, you don't want to overdo it, so just choose an additional standard to address and keep the lesson short and sweet.

Week-by-Week Homework: Reading Comprehension (Grade 3)
© Mary Rose, Scholastic Inc.

Meeting the Standards

The CCSS reading standards for literature and informational text are grouped under the umbrella of the College and Career Readiness Anchor Standards (CCR) for Reading. The chart below lists these anchor standards for grades K–5.

KEY IDEAS AND DETAILS
1. Read closely to determine what the text says explicitly and to make logical inferences from it; cite specific textual evidence when writing or speaking to support conclusions drawn from the text.
2. Determine central ideas or themes of a text and analyze their development; summarize the key supporting details and ideas.
3. Analyze how and why individuals, events, and ideas develop and interact over the course of a text.

CRAFT AND STRUCTURE
4. Interpret words and phrases as they are used in a text, including determining technical, connotative, and figurative meanings, and analyze how specific word choices shape meaning or tone.
5. Analyze the structure of texts, including how specific sentences, paragraphs, and larger portions of the text (e.g., a section, chapter, scene, or stanza) relate to each other and the whole.
6. Assess how point of view or purpose shapes the content and style of a text.

INTEGRATION OF KNOWLEDGE AND IDEAS
7. Integrate and evaluate content presented in diverse media and formats, including visually and quantitatively, as well as in words.
8. Delineate and evaluate the argument and specific claims in a text, including the validity of the reasoning as well as the relevance and sufficiency of the evidence.
9. Analyze how two or more texts address similar themes or topics in order to build knowledge or to compare the approaches the authors take.

RANGE OF READING AND LEVEL OF TEXT COMPLEXITY
10. Read and comprehend complex literary and informational texts independently and proficiently.

Week-by-Week Homework: Reading Comprehension (Grade 3)
© Mary Rose, Scholastic Inc.

The Value of Reading Aloud the Passages

Reading aloud is the best way to improve reading comprehension and fluency. Every passage in this book should be read aloud by a child to an adult for several reasons. Many families think their child reads at a much higher level than he or she actually does. Listening as a child reads aloud each week helps families develop a realistic understanding of his or her reading skills. As the school year progresses and the assignments become more difficult, families will be able to see the advances their children are making.

Classroom strategies for maximizing read-aloud experiences

The following classroom strategies are aimed at augmenting read-aloud time effectively. They will help you avoid round-robin reading and reach struggling readers.

1. **Reread familiar passages.**
   You can read a passage aloud one day and have children reread it aloud the next day. During the second reading, children will read more confidently because they understand the concept of the text and will know previously unfamiliar words.

2. **Reread old favorites.**
   Remember when you were young (or perhaps when your own children were young), and the best thing about reading was hearing the same stories over and over again? Children often get more out of a story the second or third time they hear it. Once a text becomes familiar, even struggling readers feel less self-conscious about reading aloud. When children are reading an old favorite, they tend to read more fluently.

3. **Assign special pages the day before children read them.**
   In this variation on round-robin reading, you assign each child one page to read aloud the next day. This allows time for children to focus on perfecting reading rate and vocal inflection at home, so they will be fluent when they read in front of the class.

4. **Introduce choral reading.**
   This is a particularly effective strategy for reading poetry. Try a variety of poems—poems that are funny, tell a story, have a delightful rhythm, are read in two parts, or have a deep meaning. Read the poem several times to help children feel its rhyme and get a sense of its meaning.

Week-by-Week Homework: Reading Comprehension (Grade 3)
© Mary Rose, Scholastic Inc.

5. Do paired reading.

In this technique, children read together in pairs or groups of three, scattered around the classroom. This activity is effective with both fiction and nonfiction. It fosters an environment in which children help one another understand more complicated words and concepts.

6. Read plays.

Assign roles for a play at least a day in advance. This allows children to practice their part until their reading flows fluently, and they feel comfortable with voice inflections and word meanings. Children also tend to pay extra attention when reading plays because they want to be ready when their turn to read comes.

7. Have children read their writing aloud to the class.

Build children's confidence by giving them time to read their own essays, reports, or stories aloud to the rest of the class. You can also gauge their listening skills by the kinds of questions they ask in response to hearing their peers read aloud.

Why Silent Reading Is Not Enough

As young readers build their skills, we might be tempted to allow them to complete more and more reading assignments with silent reading. Sustained, silent reading is highly effective in developing children's reading ability and increasing motivation, and children do develop their reading skills by reading. As discussed below, silent reading has its drawbacks, so it's important to make sure children are applying strategies to help them comprehend the text they're reading.

• Silent reading allows children to skip words they do not know. Skipping unfamiliar words is often taught as an effective reading strategy, and indeed it can be. But it is only a good strategy if children reread the entire sentence and try to figure out the unknown word through context or syntactic clues. We cannot tell if children are rereading for meaning when they are reading silently. Good readers may reread, but struggling readers, who need to do so the most, often may not.

• Silent reading may perpetuate children's mispronunciation of words, which hampers their comprehension of the text. When you hear children mispronounce words, use it as an opportunity to help them connect written and spoken words.

• Silent reading does not teach children to read with expression, use voice inflections, or adjust their rate of reading to reflect the content. Nor does it offer any information about the child's awareness of punctuation. When reading independently, many young readers may fail to pause for commas or quotation marks or stop for periods, which can impede their ability to make meaning of the text.

• Silent reading does not give children the opportunity to listen to themselves as they read. When children listen to themselves reading aloud, they learn to correct their errors and ensure that what they read makes sense.

Week-by-Week Homework: Reading Comprehension (Grade 3)
© Mary Rose, Scholastic Inc.

How to Simplify Your Homework Routine

The tips below will simplify yet strengthen your routine for the homework assignments in this book, as well as all the other homework you assign.

✔️ **Homework assignments should ask children to practice skills they have already mastered.**

If you're studying contractions in class today, then send home an assignment about rhyming words or another skill they learned a month ago.

✔️ **Let parents have some authority over homework assignments.**

Passing out homework assignments on Mondays and having children return their completed work by Friday of that week is a flexible and effective approach. Some children may return triumphantly on Tuesday having completed all the assignments in one night. Others may do one assignment each night. Some families may work on reading on Mondays, math on Tuesdays, and so on. Whichever scenario applies, this framework gives families control over how an assignment is completed, allowing them to schedule the work around children's other activities—scouting, sports, music, and the like—and still get the homework done on time.

✔️ **Assign appropriate homework.**

A "one-size-fits-all" assignment is not the best solution for a classroom of children with a wide range of skills. To differentiate children's assignments, label a pocket folder or large manila envelope for each child. Fill the folder or envelope with the homework assignment that matches each child's skill set. Have children turn in their folders or envelopes to you for grading.

Consider purchasing other books in this series at a variety of grade levels so you can assign pages on the same standard based on the levels of all your children.

✔️ **Give the appropriate amount of homework.**

A general guideline recommended by the National PTA is for children to have 10 minutes per night of homework per grade level. Thus, a second grader should get 20 minutes of work a night; a student in third grade should get 30 minutes of work a night.

In a typical week, your children should have one reading assignment, one math assignment, and one in science, social studies, writing, or grammar. You might also have them keep a log of what they are reading and how much time they spend doing it. Rather than producing a class chart listing the number of books children have read, which may encourage competition and exaggeration, creating individual reading logs enables you to communicate with families about the types and levels of books children choose, how much time children spend on reading, and even how many words they have to look up.

Week-by-Week Homework: Reading Comprehension (Grade 3)
© Mary Rose, Scholastic Inc.

✔ Grade homework fairly and effectively.

Families vary widely in how much assistance they provide, so rather than grading every word of every page, try giving whole credit, half credit, and no credit for assignments. You can quickly scan the completed work to see if children got the main idea of the lesson and grade accordingly: a check mark, a check minus, or an X. If a child clearly missed the point of the lesson, hold a mini-conference with him or her and allow for a "do-over."

It's also important to consider the number of homework pages a child has completed when you are deciding on a grade. Determine a total homework grade for that period and count it as if it were a score on a major test.

✔ Document the standards you have covered.

Your districts may require you to document the standards you have taught in each subject, or you may want to record that information on your own. A chart for recording information about the homework you assign appears on page 96. You can use it to mark the date you sent home an assignment and make notes about its effectiveness—especially important when you have a range of different abilities in your classroom.

Explore Scholastic's Storia website at www.scholastic.com/storia-school. Two thousand leveled eBooks—both fiction and informational texts—are available for downloading by subscription from this site. Also explore the Scholastic classroom magazines website at http://classroommagazines.scholastic.com for literary and informational text passages to share with children.

Dear Family,

I would like to ask for your assistance in helping your child become a better reader. All you have to do is complete a weekly reading homework assignment with your child. Each week, your child will bring home a short assignment: one read-aloud passage, a set of questions about the passage, and a letter with information and tips for you. Please listen to your child read the passage aloud. I encourage you to help with any difficult words. Then read the questions out loud to your child. I would like your child to answer the questions in his or her own writing. A set of guidelines for doing the assignments and helping your child improve his or her reading skills is attached.

Each lesson is specifically designed to reinforce a reading standard that your child has already learned in class. You will have all week to help your child complete this assignment, and he or she will get credit for doing the work. Please complete the bottom of the page with your signature and your child's signature to show that your child has completed the assignment.

Please contact me if you have any questions concerning this project. The first lesson is attached and is due back by _____.
Thanks for your help in making your child the best reader he or she can be!

Sincerely,

_____

Your child's teacher

Improving Your Child's Reading Skills

These guidelines will help you know when and how to assist your child as he or she reads aloud to you and then answers the questions.

Have your child read the questions before he or she reads the passage aloud. The questions on the Family Letter With Questions page are written at a higher reading level than the student passage. This simple step will provide your child with a sense of what the passage is about, tools to tackle unfamiliar names or words, and a purpose for reading. This reading will also trigger your child's background knowledge of the passage's topic.

Study the passage's title and illustrations next. These will provide even more information to set the stage for reading and help your child establish a context for words in the passage that may have more than one meaning. For instance, the passage may contain the word **bass.** If the passage is about a symphony, the word is pronounced one way; if the passage is about fishing, it is pronounced differently.

Do not immediately correct the error when your child reads a word incorrectly. The best way to improve reading comprehension and fluency is to read aloud. It is very important that you listen to your child read the passage. If your child makes an error, let him or her read to the end of the sentence. Most of the time, your child will realize that what was said aloud does not make sense and will self-correct.

If your child pauses at a word, count slowly to five. If he or she is unable to figure out the word, try one of these steps: make the sound(s) of the initial letter, refer to the illustration, or if the word has appeared previously in the passage, point it out—including different forms of the word, such as **swim** and **swam** or **baby** and **babies**. Those variations look very different to beginning readers. If your child still cannot read the word, say it. Chances are it will appear again in the passage, and your child will remember it.

Allow your child to circle or highlight words or phrases in the questions and then find the same word or phrase in the passage. Ideally, your child should be able to read the passage fluently, return to the text to find or verify the answers to the questions, and then write the answer himself or herself. If your child struggles with this, marking the text will help reinforce the idea that the answers to the questions are right there in the passage.

Help your child compose the answers to the questions. Work with your child in locating the answers and using the text to ensure correct spelling.

Some questions may require more discussion and rereading than others. The skills covered by these assignments vary greatly. Some ask children to simply recall the facts (literal questions), and some require your child to "read between the lines" and make inferences.

Week-by-Week Homework: Reading Comprehension (Grade 3)
© Mary Rose, Scholastic Inc.

Text-based answers

The Common Core State Standards (CCSS) are designed as guidelines for what children should be able to read and understand. Whether your state chooses the Partnership for Assessment of Readiness for College and Careers (PARCC) assessment, the Smarter Balanced Assessment Consortium (SBAC), or another state testing tool, CCSS assessments will measure each child's ability to understand a text and to look for answers in that text. This premise is what makes these assessments "text-based" as opposed to general knowledge and norm-referenced tests, which are often "experience-based" assessments. Background knowledge and experiences may help children understand the passages on a test but are not necessary for answering the questions.

KEY IDEAS AND DETAILS

RL.3.1 Ask and answer questions to demonstrate understanding of a text, referring explicitly to the text as the basis for the answers.

During regular classroom discussions, encourage children to cite the text when they answer questions. When young readers begin to use evidence-based terminology, they learn to find the words and ideas in the text that support their answers. Because children know they will need to return to these passages to answer questions, they become more careful and attentive readers.

We ask children to "refer to the text," but they often have difficulty deciding if they should copy a sentence, quote a character, or simply paraphrase what the author said. Teach children to look at the question for guidance. If it asks what someone said, children can respond with a direct or indirect quote: *Joey said that he was sorry for what he had done,* is an indirect quote; *Joey said, "I am sorry for what I have done,"* is a direct quote since it uses Joey's exact words and is properly punctuated. The word *that* is a magical word for children who are unsure about the proper use of commas and quotation marks.

Some children get carried away in "referring explicitly to the text" and will copy an entire sentence, or even an entire paragraph. As a general rule, they should never copy an entire paragraph. Locating information and copying it verbatim does not indicate understanding.

There are two stories for this standard. "Super Hound" has elements of science fiction in the dream that the main character has. "Ferris Wheel" is historical fiction: the characters ride on the original Ferris wheel designed and built by George Washington Gale Ferris, Jr., for the 1893 World's Columbian Exposition in Chicago and later moved to St. Louis, Missouri, for the 1904 World's Fair. "Ferris Wheel" contains questions that require children to make an inference. This inference is based on hints the author gives about the personalities of the characters without directly stating how they feel about a ride on the Ferris wheel.

15

Please send this assignment back to school by _____ .
(date)

> **Standard:** Ask and answer questions to demonstrate understanding of a text, referring explicitly to the text as the basis for the answers.

Dear Family,

The standard for this passage is simple. Your child has to demonstrate that he or she has understood the story by finding the answers to the questions below in the passage. These kinds of questions are **literal** questions because they are directly stated, and the reader doesn't have to make any inferences or draw any conclusions. For each response, please remind your child to "find where it says that in the story."

Ask your child to read the passage aloud. Then answer the questions together. When you finish, sign below.

1. What is Leo doing just before he falls asleep? _____

_____

2. Who is Super Hound? _____

_____

_____

3. How does Leo help President Jefferson? _____

_____

_____

4. What does Leo see when he wakes up? _____

_____

_____

We completed this homework assignment together.

_____   _____
(child's signature)   (family member's signature)

Week-by-Week Homework: Reading Comprehension (Grade 3)
© Mary Rose, Scholastic Inc.

Name _____ Date _____

Super Hound

by Margaret S. Gentile

Leo sat at his computer. His eyes closed sleepily as he tried to finish his book report. Suddenly Leo heard, "Leo! Wake up! I need your help!" Leo stared at the screen. A cartoon dog stared back. "I don't have time to explain," the dog said. "Touch my nose."

Leo leaned forward, touched the screen, and was pulled inside the computer. "What's going on?" he shouted. "Who are you, and why do I look like a cartoon boy now? Get me out of here!"

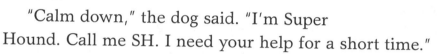

"Calm down," the dog said. "I'm Super Hound. Call me SH. I need your help for a short time."

SH took Leo to a rundown doghouse. Inside, the dog worked on a computer. "We'll use my time machine to go back in time to President Thomas Jefferson. The president thinks someone is stealing money from the government. The Louisiana Purchase will be canceled if there's not enough money in the Bank of the United States."

Leo's head whirled as they landed behind a bank building in the year 1803. SH hid inside a leather satchel that Leo carried into the bank. Leo pretended to be a reporter. He asked about the money for the Louisiana Purchase. SH crawled out of the satchel and slid under the desk.

SH poked his head back and forth. Suddenly, he jumped back into the satchel. Leo immediately said good-bye and took SH outside.

"The bank president has a desk drawer with a false bottom. I smelled freshly printed money, but I'm not sure it is real money! I'll tell Jefferson what I found. Jump in the time machine so you can go home."

Soon, Leo awoke in his own room. He saw his finished book report on "Jefferson's Challenges." What happened? Did he really travel back in time? Was it all a dream? Would he ever meet Super Hound again?

Week-by-Week Homework: Reading Comprehension (Grade 3)
© Mary Rose, Scholastic Inc.

Please send this assignment back to school by _____ .
(date)

> **Standard:** Ask and answer questions to demonstrate understanding of a text, referring explicitly to the text as the basis for the answers.

Dear Family,

In this historical fiction passage, the author reveals the personalities and fears of two children through their conversations and actions. After your child has read this story, allow him or her to pause for a moment to reflect on it. Then return to the story to find the answers to the questions below. You might encourage your child to mark the answers in the text with a pencil or crayon.

Some children have difficulty reading dialogue. Remind your child that there are three ways to know when the speakers change:

- Quotation marks enclose the words spoken by each character.
- Dialogue tags, such as "said Mark" and "whispered Margaret," identify the speaker.
- A new paragraph begins.

Ask your child to read the passage aloud. Then answer the questions together. When you finish, please sign below.

1. Where are Tommy and his family? _____

2. Which word best describes Julia: *silly, excited, scared, determined*?

_____ Why? _____

_____

3. How does the author show that Tommy might be scared? HINT: *Write two ways.*

_____

_____

4. Why does Tommy say that he loved the ride? _____

_____

We completed this homework assignment together.

_____   _____
(child's signature)   (family member's signature)

Week-by-Week Homework: Reading Comprehension (Grade 3)
© Mary Rose, Scholastic Inc.

The Ferris Wheel

Tommy looked up, up, up at the Ferris wheel, which was 264 feet high. It was the first Ferris wheel ever made. First it had been in Chicago. Now it was in St. Louis for the 1904 World's Fair. He watched the little chairs swing all the way to the top and then come back down. Tommy's stomach did a flip. He told himself that he was just excited.

"Will you ride the Ferris wheel with me, Mama?" Julia pleaded.

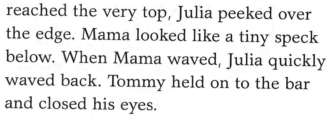

Mama shook her head. "I won't get on that thing for all the money in the world," she replied.

"Will you take me up on the Ferris wheel, Tommy?" Julia asked. "You're not scared of anything. That's what Papa says,"

"Sure, I'll take you," Tommy told Julia. "It's true. I'm not scared of anything."

Soon Tommy and Julia were sitting in a chair on the Ferris wheel. Tommy didn't say a word. He tightly gripped the bar in front of him and stared straight ahead. Julia talked and looked all around.

Tommy and Julia inched higher as each empty seat was filled with the next people in line. They looked down, down, down at the fair. When they finally reached the very top, Julia peeked over the edge. Mama looked like a tiny speck below. When Mama waved, Julia quickly waved back. Tommy held on to the bar and closed his eyes.

Then the Ferris wheel was full, and it began to turn. Music played loudly as they whooshed through the air, around and around. Each time they rose to the top, their tummies jumped.

Julia couldn't stop talking. "I'm not scared, Tommy. Don't you think this is the most beautiful ride in the world? I think I can see our farm from up here. How many more times will we get to go around?" she chattered.

In a few minutes, the Ferris wheel slowed down and then stopped. It started and stopped as the cars were loaded and unloaded. When they were at the bottom, Julia leaped from her seat. Tommy had to pry his fingers from the bar. He finally opened his eyes.

Julia ran to their mother. "It was wonderful!" she said. "We both loved the high ride, didn't we, Tommy?"

"Of course I loved it," Tommy replied. "I'm not scared of anything!"

Week-by-Week Homework: Reading Comprehension (Grade 3)
© Mary Rose, Scholastic Inc.

Recounting stories

This can be a complex standard for children in the third grade. When we ask them to recount a story, they want to share every detail instead of the most important events. Use the following mini-lesson to help children identify the most important parts of a story.

KEY IDEAS AND DETAILS

RL.3.2 Recount stories, including fables, folktales, and myths from diverse cultures; determine the central message, lesson, or moral and explain how it is conveyed through key details in the text.

Do a reading of a story that the class has read recently. Then ask children to tell you everything that happened in the story. Record their answers on a board or chart paper. As you do this, put the events in the correct order by pausing to ask where an event should go. Record exactly what children say. When you finish, ask children to help you choose the three or four main events. Circle their choices. Discuss why these are the most important ideas (they tell the main action of the plot) and the others are less important details. Finish the lesson by emphasizing to children that when they retell a story, they should include the most important events and leave out the details.

Determining the theme or message

The passage for this standard is a French folktale that has some parallels to Cinderella. This three-step plan shows how to help children determine the central message, lesson, or moral of the story: 1) Have children select one word to describe the story. 2) Ask them to use that word in a sentence about the story. 3) Then ask children to use story details to relate their sentence to a life lesson. For example, a child might offer the word *kind* to describe the story, then produce this sentence: "When people are kind, nice things happen to them." Supportive details that link to a life lesson could be, "The young girl was kind to everyone, and she got to marry the handsome prince. The lesson of this story is to be kind to everyone." The chart below contains common themes in children's literature.

Home: family relationships; happy ending	**Good and evil:** good guys versus bad guys
Hope: looking forward to the future	**Teamwork:** working together to achieve great things
Friendship: being a true and loyal friend	**Kindness:** the rewards of being generous and considerate
Honesty: telling the truth	**Helpfulness:** helping others and recognizing those who help us
Family: cherish family ties	**Nature:** the connection between nature/animals/pets/self

Week-by-Week Homework: Reading Comprehension (Grade 3)
© Mary Rose, Scholastic Inc.

Please send this assignment back to school by _____ .
(date)

> **Standard:** Recount stories, including fables, folktales, and myths from diverse cultures; determine the central message, lesson, or moral and explain how it is conveyed through key details in the text.

Dear Family,

   After your child has read this story to you, see if he or she can retell the tale, which is the first part of this standard. The second skill is for your child to identify the moral or lesson of the story, which is revealed by the vastly different actions and words of the two daughters. To help your child determine the moral for question 3, ask what lesson he or she has learned from this story of the two girls. What was the final outcome for both girls and how might that apply to your child's life?

Ask your child to read the passage aloud. Then answer the questions together. When you finish, please sign below.

1. How does the mother feel about her daughter Emma? _____

_____

Which sentence in the passage best supports this answer? _____

_____

2. Why doesn't the woman at the well give the same gift to both girls? _____

_____

3. What is the moral or lesson of this story? (What lesson did you learn from it?)

_____

_____

4. What words in the story tell you that this is a folktale? _____

_____

We completed this homework assignment together.

_____   _____
(child's signature)   (family member's signature)

Week-by-Week Homework: Reading Comprehension (Grade 3)
© Mary Rose, Scholastic Inc.

Jewels and Toads: A French Folktale

Once upon a time, a woman had two daughters. Mila, the older one, was mean and selfish, like her mother. The younger girl, Emma, was gentle and kind. The mother loved her older daughter more, so she treated Mila well. She made Emma work hard and walk a mile to the well to get fresh water.

One day, Emma saw a poor, ragged woman at the well. The woman begged the child for a drink. Emma gave the woman some water to drink. The ragged woman was weak so Emma carefully held the pitcher for her.

"You are so kind," said the woman. "I will give you a gift. From now on, every time you speak, a jewel will fall from your mouth."

When Emma returned home, her mother scolded her for being gone for so long. "I am so sorry, mother," said Emma. When Emma spoke, a diamond came out of her mouth.

Her mother was surprised, but she quickly caught the jewel. "How does this happen, my dear, sweet, favorite child?" she asked.

Emma told her mother about the woman at the well. The next morning, the mother sent Mila to get water. She was sure the old woman would give Mila the same gift.

The poor, ragged woman was at the well. She asked Mila for a drink. "No. You're just an ugly, old beggar woman. Just give me the same gift you gave my sister," Mila demanded.

"I'll give you a gift," the woman muttered.

When Mila spoke, a toad tumbled out of her mouth. Her mother was very surprised, and she didn't catch the toad. "You have caused this," the mother screamed at Emma. "You must leave this house at once and never come back."

Emma left the house and went into the woods. There, she saw the king's son. "Why are you all alone in these woods?" the prince asked.

When Emma told him what happened, jewels fell from her mouth. The prince took her home to meet his family. They were soon married and lived happily ever after.

Character analysis and inferences

Authors go to great lengths to develop characters and imbue them with specific traits. When we read books in a series that feature the same main character, we may actually feel as if we know this character and can predict their words and actions.

> ### KEY IDEAS AND DETAILS
>
> RL.3.3 Describe characters in a story (e.g., their traits, motivations, or feelings) and explain how their actions contribute to the sequence of events.

Third graders are still learning to understand literature; they often don't make inferences that would help them understand the actions of a character. The activity below uses a book from James Marshall's Miss Nelson series to help develop children's inferencing skills.

Ask, "What kind of character is Miss Nelson in *Miss Nelson Is Missing?*" Children might say she was kind, pretty, tricky, nosy, secretive, or clever. (Note that none of these words appears in the book.) Then ask, "Why do you think Miss Nelson was tricky?" The response will be the justification for the inference that she's tricky. This is actually very high-level thinking and is ranked at the top of Bloom's Taxonomy. Eventually children should be able to make inferences about almost any character by writing, "I think _____ is _____ because . . ."

Character traits determine the outcome of the plot

In *Miss Nelson Is Missing*, the traits and actions of the main character are the focus of the plot. As the activity above reveals, Miss Nelson is tricky—her actions contribute to the outcome of the plot—and her trick remains a secret. The passage for this standard is "Anansi, the Firefly, and the Tiger," a retelling of an African folktale featuring a particularly greedy main character. This greediness has an effect on how the events play out for the character.

Evidence-Based Selected Response (EBSR)

Assessments designed to test children's proficiency on the CCSS, such as the Partnership for Assessment of Readiness for College and Careers (PARCC) test, contain evidence-based selected response (EBSR) questions. These questions have two parts. Part A is a multiple-choice question that often has more than one correct answer. In Part B, children must identify a detail from the text that best supports their answer to Part A. If children answer Part A incorrectly, they do not receive credit for a correct response on Part B.

Even if your third graders do not take the PARCC assessment, exposing them to these kinds of complex questions will help them become more careful readers and more critical thinkers.

Please send this assignment back to school by _____ .
(date)

> **Standard:** Describe characters in a story (e.g., their traits, motivations, or feelings) and explain how their actions contribute to the sequence of events.

Dear Family,

In this assignment, your child will describe the main character in the passage, Anansi, and determine how his personality contributes to the events in the plot. Anansi's personality is hinted at without using adjectives to describe him. The author does this by describing Anansi's actions and feelings.

After listening to your child read the passage aloud, share the adage, "Actions speak louder than words." See if he or she can relate this to the passage.

In question 1, your child should circle two words as answers in Part A and write only one sentence in Part B. That sentence should be copied directly from the story and demonstrate why the choice in Part A is a solid one.

Ask your child to read the passage aloud. Then answer the questions together. When you finish, please sign below.

1. **Part A:** Circle the two words that best describe Anansi.

   a. sad   **b.** sneaky   **c.** slow   **d.** amusing   **e.** greedy   **f.** friendly

   Part B: Find a sentence in the passage that supports one of your responses to Part A. _____

2. How does the moral of the story apply to Anansi? Use details from the story to explain your answer. _____
_____

3. Why does Anansi say there must be fleas in Tiger's house? _____
_____

We completed this homework assignment together.

_____   _____
(child's signature)   (family member's signature)

Name _____ Date _____

Anansi, the Firefly, and the Tiger: An African Folktale Retold

Anansi was a spider—and not a very nice spider at that. He always played tricks on other animals and then laughed at their bad luck.

One night, Firefly asked Anansi to go egg hunting with him. Firefly used the beautiful, golden glow of his tail so Anansi could find lots of eggs.

Each time Anansi found an egg, he screamed, "This one is for me!" He dropped the egg into his basket. Poor Firefly had no eggs in her basket at all.

On the way home, Anansi and Firefly stopped to visit Tiger. Tiger saw the basket full of eggs and offered to cook them for supper. Anansi was very happy about this. He did not like raw eggs.

As Tiger and his family ate many of the hard-boiled eggs, Anansi stared at their sharp teeth and huge claws. He was afraid to eat any eggs, even though he felt they belonged to him.

Tiger invited the tiny animals to spend the night. When it was dark, Tiger put a lobster in a pot with the rest of the eggs. He covered it with some broken eggshells. Anansi decided to trick Tiger and eat all the leftover eggs. He thought they were his anyway, so he should not have to share.

Anansi reached into the pot. The lobster pinched Anansi, and he screamed. Firefly and Tiger came running. "What are you doing, Anansi?" Tiger asked.

"There must be fleas in this house," explained Anansi. "One of them has bitten me."

"How dare you say I have fleas," roared Tiger. He began to chase Anansi. We all know how fast a spider can run when he is being chased. Anansi escaped and ran to his own house. Then Tiger invited Firefly to have a late-night snack of hard-boiled eggs.

Moral of the story: Those who are greedy often end up with nothing.

Week-by-Week Homework: Reading Comprehension (Grade 3)
© Mary Rose, Scholastic Inc.

Literal and nonliteral language

Literal language means exactly what it says: *The pill was a quarter of an inch wide.* Nonliteral language goes beyond the dictionary meaning of words. Words and phrases or ideas often bring emphasis or humor to the writing and are used to help readers picture a situation: *The pill was so large that swallowing it felt like swallowing an elephant!*

CRAFT AND STRUCTURE

RL.3.4 Determine the meaning of words and phrases as they are used in a text, distinguishing literal from nonliteral language.

By grade 3, children are just beginning to understand humor, like knock-knock jokes and puns. Young readers realize that words do not always mean exactly what they say. Once children figure out this play of words, they can almost drive you crazy with jokes and their own special brand of eight-year-old humor.

For children who have learning disabilities or are learning a new language, figurative, nonliteral language is mystifying. Help children understand nonliteral language by using it often in your conversations with them, and then pausing for a 30-second discussion of what you actually mean.

"The Dragon and the Stone" contains wonderful nonliteral language to describe the forest, the price of a popular stone, and the weight—and fate—of a dragon.

Context clues

Context clues can give readers hints about the meaning of a familiar word used in an unfamiliar way. What do we, as literate adults, do when we read something that does not make sense? First, we reread the sentence to get the syntax of the word; we determine if it is a noun, adjective, verb, or an adverb. (*Bass* as a fish is a noun; *bass* as a description of a person's voice is an adjective.) The clue is the way the word is used in a sentence—its context.

We may even have to read the sentence a third time and skip the word. We may try substituting a different word to see if it might make sense. ("He pulled in the bass" could be read as "He pulled in the fish.") If we still do not know the word, we read the sentences around it or glance at an illustration or another text feature. In the example above, we might know that the person is in a boat and that she has a rod, reel, and bait. All of these clues, plus the word's usage in the sentence, are context clues to help us quickly conclude that *bass* refers to a fish.

Please send this assignment back to school by _____ .
(date)

> **Standard:** Determine the meaning of words and phrases as they are used in a text, distinguishing literal from nonliteral language.

Dear Family,

Literal language uses words that mean exactly what they say: **The pill was a quarter of an inch wide.** Nonliteral language is when words go beyond their meaning in the dictionary to convey an idea: **Swallowing that pill felt like I was swallowing an elephant!**

For this assignment, your child will need to interpret the meaning of the **boldface** nonliteral phrases in the passage. Have your child pause and use his or her own words to tell you what these phrases mean.

Ask your child to read the passage aloud. Then answer the questions together. When you finish, please sign below.

What does each sentence from the passage mean? Circle the correct answer.

1. "It holds misery and sadness."

   a. The forest is a dangerous place.   **b.** It is dark and gloomy in the forest.

   c. Only unhappy people visit the forest.   **d.** People get lost in the forest.

2. "This stone she could sell for a handsome price."

   a. Pieces of gold are pretty because they shine.

   b. The stone wasn't worth very much money.

   c. A good-looking person would buy the stone.

   d. She could get a lot of money for the stone.

3. "The ground broke under his weight."

   a. The ground was too soft and wet.   **b.** The dragon fell into a large hole.

   c. The dragon's feet sank in the ground.   **d.** The ground was covered with stones.

We completed this homework assignment together.

_____
(child's signature)

_____
(family member's signature)

Week-by-Week Homework: Reading Comprehension (Grade 3)
© Mary Rose, Scholastic Inc.

Name _____   Date _____

The Dragon and the Stone

by Margaret S. Gentile

Long ago, there was a beautiful wood filled with flowers, streams, and animals. Then a cruel dragon named Vindred came to rule the forest. Soon, the forest was covered in thick, gray smoke, and those who entered never returned. Anyone who looked into the eyes of the dragon instantly turned into stone. That is how Marta's father disappeared. He and nine other men had tried to fight the dragon and save the forest. Since then, Marta's mother warned her: "Do not go into the forest. **It holds misery and sadness."**

Marta was careful to stay away from the woods—until one day. She was gathering pretty stones to sell at the market. Marta was lucky to find a piece of mica, a shiny thin rock used for making jewelry.

This stone she could sell for a handsome price! She gently rubbed the stone to make it shine even more. She gazed at its beauty as she walked. Without knowing it, Marta wandered into the forest. She soon met Vindred.

Marta was so scared she fell to her knees. She could feel the heat of Vindred's breath. **The ground broke under his weight.** "I shall turn you into stone!" the dragon roared.

Vindred lowered his head to force Marta to look into his terrible eyes. Marta buried her head in her cape and bravely held up her hand. She flashed the shining mica into the dragon's face. As he looked at his own reflection, the curse swallowed the terrible beast. With a loud shriek Vindred yelled, "Fool! Fool! What have you done? This cannot—" He stopped suddenly, for he had turned to stone.

Immediately, the woods changed. The gray smoke sank into the ground. Everywhere, the plants turned green. Flowers of all colors bloomed, and animals appeared as if they were waking from sleep. Then from out of the forest came ten men. Marta's once-lost father hugged her and led everyone home.

Week-by-Week Homework: Reading Comprehension (Grade 3)
© Mary Rose, Scholastic Inc.

Using plays in the classroom

One way to improve children's reading comprehension and fluency is to have them read out loud—and what better way to do this than by having them read plays and act the parts.

The passage for this standard is an adaptation of "The Elephant's Child" from Rudyard Kipling's *Just So Stories*. Before you send this assignment home, make sure that children understand the meaning of "bulgy nose" and "'satiable curtiosity" (insatiable curiosity) and that they can mimic the muffled, distorted voice of the little elephant when the Crocodile is pulling his nose.

CRAFT AND STRUCTURE

RL.3.5 Refer to parts of stories, dramas, and poems when writing or speaking about a text, using terms such as chapter, script, and stanza; describe how each successive part builds on earlier sections.

Terms for plays

Introduce the following terms that apply to dramas:

Script: contains a list of characters, stage directions, and dialogue

Setting: where and when the play happens

Props: objects that a character uses or talks about

Acts: the main parts of a play

Scenes: parts of an act; each scene tells a particular part of the play

Rising action: the events in the plot that lead to the climax

Climax: the turning point of the play when the action is at its height, often the most exciting scene

Plot: the events in the play

Protagonist: the main character in the play

Storyworks magazine from Scholastic (storyworks.scholastic.com) is a good source for plays. You can also search Scholastic's Teacher Store website (shop.scholastic.com) for plays on many topics.

Week-by-Week Homework: Reading Comprehension (Grade 3)
© Mary Rose, Scholastic Inc.

> **Standard:** Refer to parts of stories, dramas, and poems when writing or speaking about a text, using terms such as chapter, script, and stanza; describe how each successive part builds on earlier sections.

Dear Family,

The pattern in "The Elephant's Child" is a familiar one—two or three encounters between characters set up the main action of the play. This is called the "rising action." Help your child make this distinction by noting what action takes place in each act.

Your child should also understand terms such as **narrator**, **main character**, and **plot**, and how those terms apply to plays as well as to poetry or fiction.

Part of this play is written in dialect. Some words are intentionally abbreviated or misspelled to reflect the way they might have been spoken by the character.

Ask your child to read the passage aloud. Then answer the questions together. When you finish, please sign below.

1. Who is the main character in this play? _____

2. In which act does the Elephant's Child first display his 'satiable curtiosity?

_____

3. What is the job of the narrator in the play? _____

4. In Act 3, why does the Crocodile tell the Elephant's Child to come closer?

_____

5. Part A: What does "'satiable curtiosity" mean?

    a. thinking about food all the time   **b.** happening only in the jungle

    c. looking for something that is lost   **d.** wanting to know everything

    Part B: Find a sentence in the passage that supports your response to Part A.

_____

We completed this homework assignment together.

_____   _____
(child's signature)   (family member's signature)

The Elephant's Child

Narrator: In the High and Far-Off Times, the elephant had no trunk. He had only a little bulgy nose. One elephant, the Elephant's Child, was full of 'satiable curtiosity. He asked ever so many questions.

Act 1: on the African plains

Elephant's Child: Ostrich, why do your tail feathers grow just so?

Ostrich: You ask too many questions! Stop asking questions all day long!

Elephant's Child: Giraffe, what makes your skin so spotty?

Giraffe: You ask too many questions! Stop asking questions all day long!

Elephant's Child: Hippopotamus, why are your eyes so red?

Hippopotamus: You ask too many questions! Stop asking questions all day long!

Act 2: on the African plains

Narrator: No one would answer the Elephant's Child's questions, but he still had 'satiable curtiosity. He began to wonder about the Crocodile, which he had never seen.

Elephant's Child: Kolokolo Bird, what does the Crocodile have for dinner?

Kolokolo Bird: Go to the banks of the great, gray-green, greasy Limpopo River and find out!

Narrator: The next morning the Elephant's Child set out for the banks of the great, gray-green, greasy Limpopo River to find the Crocodile.

Act 3: on the banks of the Limpopo River

Elephant's Child: 'Scuse me, but have you seen the Crocodile around here?

Crocodile: Well, I am the Crocodile.

Elephant's Child: What do you have for dinner?

Crocodile: Come closer, and I'll whisper.

Narrator: The Elephant's Child put his head down close to the Crocodile's musky, tusky mouth—and the Crocodile caught him by his little bulgy nose.

Crocodile: I'll have Elephant for dinner!

Elephant's Child: Led go! You are hurtig be!

Narrator: The Crocodile pulled, and the Elephant's Child pulled. The Elephant Child's nose got longer and longer. At last the Crocodile let go, but the Elephant's Child's nose stayed very, very long.

After that, the Elephant's Child used his trunk to pull fruit off trees. He picked up grass with his trunk. He swished biting flies away with his trunk. Soon, the other elephants went to the banks of the great, gray-green, greasy Limpopo River. The crocodile gave each one a very, very long nose, too.

Week-by-Week Homework: Reading Comprehension (Grade 3)
© Mary Rose, Scholastic Inc.

Differing points of view

In order to master this standard, children must first be able to understand who is telling the story. Then they can delve into how the story might change if another character or narrator told it and whether they agree with the author's message. Although the narrator of each poem in "What Is the Best Fruit?"

CRAFT AND STRUCTURE

RL.3.6 Distinguish their own point of view from that of the narrator or those of the characters.

is unnamed, his or her point of view is clearly stated. After reading the poems, children can address the standard by comparing their own point of view with the poet's in an activity like the one below.

Identifying points of view in the poems

Before you send this assignment home, work with children to create a graph showing which of four kinds of fruit is their personal favorite. Help them read the graph by asking which fruit is the favorite in the class, which is the least favorite, and if any fruits received the same number of votes.

As children read "What Is the Best Fruit?" they should notice that each poem is a vote for a favorite fruit and that the poet gives reasons why each fruit is the best. After this lesson has been completed and returned to you, allow children to write their own poems about fruit. They can use these poems as a template and simply change the fruit, or they can write their own apple, banana, or grape poem.

Rhyming patterns

The poems also provide an opportunity to help children find rhyming patterns. They will not know terms like *iambic pentameter* or recognize rhyming patterns like ABAB, but if they use crayons to circle the rhyming words at the end of each line, they will quickly see the following patterns:

"Apples": The last words in the first and second lines rhyme; the last words in the third and fourth lines rhyme.

"Bananas": The last words in the second and fourth lines rhyme.

"Grapes": There are no rhymes since it is free verse. Emphasize that not all poems rhyme.

If you ask children to write their own poems, suggest that they circle the words that rhyme and see if their pattern matches any of those in the homework poems.

Week-by-Week Homework: Reading Comprehension (Grade 3)
© Mary Rose, Scholastic Inc.

Please send this assignment back to school by _____ .
(date)

> **Standard:** Distinguish their own point of view from that of the narrator or those of the characters.

Dear Family,

These poems were written to express an opinion about the merits of three different kinds of fruit. The standard in this assignment asks your child to distinguish his or her point of view from that of the poet. (With which poem does he or she agree or disagree?)

Notice that two of the poems have rhyming patterns and a different cadence or meter. "Grapes" is a free verse poem and does not rhyme at all. To help your child see the pattern of rhyming words in the other poems, have him or her use different colors of crayons and circle the pairs of words that rhyme in matching colors.

Ask your child to read the passage aloud. Then answer the questions together. When you finish, please sign below.

1. Which poem tells the greatest number of ways to eat that fruit? _____

_____

2. According to the poems, which fruit is used to make raisins? _____

_____

3. Each poem tells why a particular fruit is best. Which poem does the best job of

convincing you that it is the best fruit? Tell why. _____

_____

_____

_____

We completed this homework assignment together.

_____   _____
(child's signature)   (family member's signature)

Week-by-Week Homework: Reading Comprehension (Grade 3)
© Mary Rose, Scholastic Inc.

Name _____   Date _____

What Is the Best Fruit?

Apples

I don't care what the rest of you say,
The best fruit of all is an apple a day.
Hot caramel gooey, dipped candy red,
In pie or a dumpling—that's what I said.

Applesauce, yum, all cinnamony sweet.
Baked apple cobbler, now that is a treat.
Fried, baked, or raw, cold, crisp in the fall,
An apple, an apple is the best fruit of all.

Bananas

Bananas in a pudding,
Bananas in a dish,
Bananas on a chocolate stick,
Any way you wish.

Bananas are the best fruit,
I know you will agree,
Bananas are such fun to eat,
Come share yours with ME!

Grapes

How can grapes not be the best fruit of all?
They are so delicious dipped in sugar and then frozen.
What a dessert!
And grape juice?
There to greet me in the morning
and give me a purple mustache
to wear to school.

Did you know that all kinds of things
are made from grapes?
Grape jelly and jam, and
You are not going to believe this—RAISINS!

Week-by-Week Homework: Reading Comprehension (Grade 3)
© Mary Rose, Scholastic Inc.

Using illustrations to understand the story

By the third grade, most children are reading chapter books with very few illustrations. That does not mean that those illustrations are insignificant. Illustrations, especially those on a book cover, can give us a sense of what lies inside the text and what kind of book it is. For instance, think of the simple drawings on the cover of *Diary of a Wimpy Kid* by Jeff Kinney. They immediately convey a feeling of whimsy and humor. On the other hand, the dark, foreboding covers of the Series of Unfortunate Events books by Lemony Snicket tell us that these stories have dark themes with little humor.

INTEGRATION OF KNOWLEDGE AND IDEAS

RL.3.7 Explain how specific aspects of a text's illustrations contribute to what is conveyed by the words in a story (e.g., create mood, emphasize aspects of a character or setting).

As this standard states, illustrations contribute greatly to the words in a story. They can create a mood (scary, happy, silly, mysterious) or hint at a setting (the old West, outer space, medieval times, a classroom, a circus). Sometimes the illustrations give us clues about a character, too. How is the face of Dracula drawn? What clothes do the students in the Harry Potter series wear? How does the artist make us think that Mrs. Piggle-Wiggle is a happy, jolly, helpful neighbor?

The illustration with "The Trojan Horse," the passage for this standard, shows the immense size of the gift—and how so many men could have concealed themselves inside it.

Lesson ideas for using illustrations

You can help children become more aware of the value of illustrations in a text by doing the following activities.

• Read a short story aloud without showing any illustrations to children or giving any clues about the setting. Then ask each child to interpret what he or she heard by creating a cover or a poster for the story. The results are usually delightful and worthy of a bulletin board display.

• Take a trip to the school library or to your classroom library. Randomly pull out a few books, hide their titles, and then show the covers. Ask children if they think the book might be funny, sad, happy, silly, or scary and what it might be about. This is great to do with picture books, of course, but it's also fun with chapter books. Just looking at intriguing covers will teach children how to "judge a book by its cover," and it might entice them to read a book they might not have selected otherwise.

> **Standard:** Explain how specific aspects of a text's illustrations contribute to what is conveyed by the words in a story (e.g., create mood, emphasize aspects of a character or setting).

Dear Family,

This standard asks children to use the information contained in an illustration to help understand a story. In "The Trojan Horse," the illustration shows the setting and emphasizes the size of the wooden horse.

The questions below also ask your child to list the steps the Greeks took to trick the Trojans. This will show that your child understands the story and the chronological order of events.

Ask your child to read the passage aloud. Then answer the questions together. When you finish, please sign below.

1. How many Greeks were inside the Trojan Horse? _____

2. Why did the Trojans take the statue into their city? _____

_____

_____

3. Write in order the steps the Greeks used to trick the Trojans and win the war.

_____

_____

_____

4. What is the meaning of the phrase, "Beware of Greeks bearing gifts?"

_____

_____

We completed this homework assignment together.

_____   _____
(child's signature)   (family member's signature)

Week-by-Week Homework: Reading Comprehension (Grade 3)
© Mary Rose, Scholastic Inc.

The Trojan Horse

The Trojans were fighting the Greeks. This war had lasted for ten years. Still, the Greeks could not get inside the walls of the Trojans' city, Troy. They could not win the war.

Then, the Greeks suddenly packed up and sailed away. Before they left, the Greeks even burned their tents. It looked like the war was finally over, and the Trojans were the winners. The only thing the Greeks left behind was a statue of a huge wooden horse. The horse was the symbol of the city of Troy, like the mascot for a sports team today. Most Trojans were pleased with this gift. They brought the statue into the city.

But the Trojan priest, Laocoön [lay-A-kuh-wahn], was *not* pleased. He thought the wooden horse might be a trick. He said, "I fear Greeks, even those bearing gifts." Laocoön did not think the statue should be brought into the city. He wondered why the enemy would leave a gift behind.

The Trojans should have listened to Laocoön. That night, 40 men from the Greek army climbed out of the giant wooden horse. They were joined by the rest of their army who had sailed back to Troy in the darkness. Suddenly, there were hundreds of Greeks inside the city of Troy. They burned and destroyed the city. The Greeks had finally won the Trojan War.

Today, you may hear the phrase, "Beware of Greeks bearing gifts." This means that you should not trust an enemy who is suddenly nice to you. The term "Trojan horse" refers to a trick that gets someone to bring an enemy into a protected place.

Week-by-Week Homework: Reading Comprehension (Grade 3)
© Mary Rose, Scholastic Inc.

Lesson ideas for comparing themes, settings, and plots

- Begin a mini-unit by reading aloud the first book in a series. Classic series, such as The Boxcar Children by Gertrude Chandler Warner and Encyclopedia Brown by Donald J. Sobol, or new series such as Shredderman by Wendelin Van Draanen (a great series that deals with bullying) or Meg Mackintosh by Lucinda Landon, are perfect for this age group.

INTEGRATION OF KNOWLEDGE AND IDEAS

RL.3.9 Compare and contrast the themes, settings, and plots of stories written by the same author about the same or similar characters (e.g., in books from a series).

  After you have read the first book, make a chart to display in the classroom. At the top of the chart, write these column headings: *Title, Setting, Main Characters, Secondary Characters, Plot, Theme,* and *Ending.* Ask children to tell you what to write in each column. Then ask them to read another book by the same author, preferably with the same protagonist.

  If you are fortunate enough to have class sets of books, give each child a copy of the same book and spend the next week or so reading it aloud in class. You can read parts of it yourself to speed up the process. I recommend that you read the first chapter aloud to engage children in the story.

  If you have a limited number of copies of the same title, use books from this series when you work with children in small groups. When the group has finished the book, add the information to the chart. After children are familiar with adding information to the chart, have them read books from the series independently and write the data from their book on the chart.

- Use the chart to address the standard. Discuss the similarities in theme, setting, and plot in the series. Before you expect children to write independent sentences or paragraphs that compare these literary elements, make sure you model how to do this for the class. If this will be difficult for children, allow them to work in small groups or pairs to complete a comparison paragraph before they write one independently.

Paired passages

Children will encounter paired passages in many testing situations. They will be asked to compare and contrast the characters, settings, plots, and themes. The first assignment for this standard is a pair of fables adapted from Aesop. Both feature a wise mouse as the main character, and each leaves readers with a lesson about bravery. The second assignment features a pair of passages based on King Arthur's exploits.

Please send this assignment back to school by _____ .
(date)

> **Standard:** Compare and contrast the themes, settings, and plots of stories written by the same author about the same or similar characters (e.g., in books from a series).

Dear Family,

The two passages for this assignment are adapted from Aesop's fables. Your child will identify the similarities and differences between the two fables and determine the lesson they learn from each one.

Aesop's fables are about 2,500 years old, yet their timeless lessons have survived and serve us well even today. After your child reads each fable to you and after you complete the questions below, take a few minutes to reflect on how the lessons of these passages might apply to your child's everyday life.

Ask your child to read the passage aloud. Then answer the questions together. When you finish, please sign below.

1. Who is the main character in each fable? _____

_____

2. What is the lesson of "The Council of Mice"? _____

_____

3. How does the lion help the mouse? _____

4. How does the mouse help the lion? _____

5. What is the lesson of the "The Lion and the Mouse?" _____

_____

_____

We completed this homework assignment together.

_____   _____
(child's signature)   (family member's signature)

Week-by-Week Homework: Reading Comprehension (Grade 3)
© Mary Rose, Scholastic Inc.

Name _____   Date _____

The Council of Mice

Long ago, the mice held a council to decide what they could do about their enemy, the Cat. They talked and talked, but no one could think of a good way to keep themselves safe from the cat's claws and sharp teeth.

Finally, a young mouse had an idea. "We need something that will tell us when the cat is near," she suggested. "Then we will have time to hide and be safe."

"What do you have in mind?" asked a wise old mouse.

"What if we tie a bell around the neck of the cat? When he is near us, we will hear it ring," she replied.

"That is a wonderful idea," said the wise old mouse. "Now I have just one question for you: Who will bell the cat?"

Name _____ Date _____

The Lion and the Mouse

Long ago, a lion was sleeping when a tiny mouse ran across his paw. The lion suddenly awoke and picked the mouse up by her tail. He was ready to eat her in one gulp. "Please spare me, oh Lion," begged the mouse. "I am so tiny. I am not a proper meal for you."

"I am King of the Beasts. It is my duty to eat you," replied the Lion in a deep voice.

"I know you are the King of the Beasts. If you would please spare my life, perhaps someday I can be of service to you," the tiny mouse answered.

The lion roared and laughed and laughed and roared again. "There is no way a tiny mouse can help me, but I will spare your life anyway."

Days passed. The little mouse was on her way home when she heard a roar of pain. She looked up in the trees to see the King of the Beasts caught in a rope trap. "Lion, I have not forgotten your kindness to me," said the little mouse. "I will help you now."

The mouse climbed the tree and began to chew the ropes. She chewed and chewed and chewed until, at last, the ropes fell away, and the lion was free.

Week-by-Week Homework: Reading Comprehension (Grade 3)
© Mary Rose, Scholastic Inc.

Please send this assignment back to school by _____ .
(date)

> **Standard:** Compare and contrast the themes, settings, and plots of stories written by the same author about the same or similar characters (e.g., in books from a series).

Dear Family,

For this assignment, your child will compare and contrast the settings, characters, and themes of two stories adapted from the same source, **King Arthur and the Knights of the Round Table**. Both are set in medieval England.

For question 2, help your child select a theme and write a sentence to explain why it is a good choice. You are welcome to come up with your own theme, too—as long as you and your child can find details from the stories to justify your choice.

Your child may be unfamiliar with some of the words in the story, such as **sorcerer**, **encouraged**, and **defeat.** Help him or her pronounce these words and talk about their meanings.

Ask your child to read the passage aloud. Then answer the questions together. When you finish, please sign below.

1. Which characters are in both stories? _____

2. Here is a list of themes that these stories share: *magic, royalty, having someone look after you, destiny, myth, medieval times, loyalty.* Choose one (or write your own!) and tell why it is a good theme for both stories.

_____

_____

3. Name one difference between the two stories. _____

_____

4. What two jobs does Merlin have in these stories? _____

_____

We completed this homework assignment together.

_____ _____
(child's signature)   (family member's signature)

Name _____   Date _____

The Sword in the Stone

After Uther Pendragon died, England needed a new king. Uther Pendragon didn't have any sons, so there could be no king. Merlin, a sorcerer, came up with a magic plan. He set a large stone outside a church in London. A sword was stuck in the stone. The handle of the sword glittered with precious jewels. Written at the bottom of the stone were these words: "*Whoever pulls this sword out of the stone shall be the King of England.*"

Soon, men from all over England were coming to London to try to pull the sword out of the stone. No one succeeded. Not even the strongest men in the country could free the sword.

A few years later, Sir Ector decided that his son Sir Kay should try to pull the sword out of the stone. Arthur, Sir Ector's adopted son, watched. Sir Kay pulled with all his strength. The sword didn't move.

Merlin stood in the crowd, watching. He moved close to Arthur. "Why don't you try to pull the sword out of the stone?" Merlin suggested.

Sir Ector and Sir Kay laughed. Merlin didn't smile. He was serious. Arthur walked up to the sword. He grabbed the handle. Before anyone knew what had happened—or how it had happened—Arthur easily freed the sword from the stone.

Everyone was amazed. Only the man who was to become King of England had the power to pull the sword from the stone. The people knelt and bowed to King Arthur. They had a leader at last! "Long live the king!" they cheered.

Week-by-Week Homework: Reading Comprehension (Grade 3)
© Mary Rose, Scholastic Inc.

The Lady of the Lake

The sorcerer, Merlin, had been King Arthur's tutor for 15 years. He encouraged the young king to enjoy himself but to stay close to home. One night, Sir Roland, Sir Kay, and King Arthur went out for a ride.

They were soon in danger, surrounded by 12 enemies. They fought bravely for a while. When Arthur raised his sword, the enemy's leader smashed it into 20 pieces. King Arthur, Sir Roland, and Sir Kay were badly wounded and in danger of dying.

All of a sudden, the enemies became frightened and began to shake. They covered their eyes in terror and ran away.

The three men looked up to see Merlin. They wondered what kind of magic the sorcerer had used to scare off their enemies. It was lucky that Merlin had come to find the men and keep them safe. Still, King Arthur was upset about losing his sword. He was King of England because of that sword.

Merlin told Arthur not to worry. He took the king to a lake where they saw a beautiful woman walking out of the water. She held a sword. "I am the Lady of the Lake," she said. "This sword is called Excalibur. As long as it is yours, King Arthur, you shall never know defeat. You will never lose to your enemy."

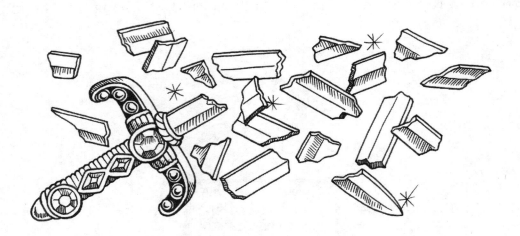

Week-by-Week Homework: Reading Comprehension (Grade 3)
© Mary Rose, Scholastic Inc.

Citing the text

Notice that the standard says, "referring explicitly to the text as the basis for the answers." When children are answering questions about a text, encourage them to use these phrases to show how and where they found information for their responses: "The author says . . ." "According to the text . . ." "It says on page . . ." "From my reading, I know that . . ."

KEY IDEAS AND DETAILS

RI.3.1 Ask and answer questions to demonstrate understanding of a text, referring explicitly to the text as the basis for the answers.

Substitutes for the term "passage"

Children may encounter a variety of terms for written work on standardized tests: *passage, selection, piece, text, article* (for an informational or narrative text), and *story* (for a literary text). Check the sample tests for your district and state to see which terms are used. Make sure children understand that those terms refer to a reading passage on which they are being tested. This may seem like a simple, logical concept that you should not have to teach, but you should cover it anyway. If it helps just a few of your struggling readers get questions correct, it is worth the classroom time.

Technology-Enhanced Constructed Response (TECR)

While we are teaching children to read and write, remember that to pass new nationwide assessments, they must also demonstrate some computer skills. The Partnership for Assessment of Readiness for College and Careers (PARCC) refers to these skills as Technology-Enhanced Constructed Response (TECR). Because some new assessments are computer-based, children will be asked to perform the following actions to enter an answer: *drag and drop, move items to show relationships,* and *cut and paste.*

Children may have to perform these functions to indicate chronological order or to sequence events or order the steps in a process, such as the parts of a life cycle. They may have to fill in blanks to complete sentences, or to write information in charts, or shade text to identify supporting details or identify a character's trait or characteristic.

Week-by-Week Homework: Reading Comprehension (Grade 3)
© Mary Rose, Scholastic Inc.

Please send this assignment back to school by _____ .
(date)

> **Standard:** Ask and answer questions to demonstrate understanding of a text, referring explicitly to the text as the basis for the answers.

Dear Family,

   All the questions below are text-based or literal questions, which means their answers can be found directly in the text. Your child should be able to answer the questions correctly even if he or she has never seen a Dalmatian dog. To refer to the text, your child can use such phrases as, "The article says . . ." "In the second paragraph . . ." "I can tell by my reading that . . ." For this assignment, your child should not copy the text exactly, but should put the information in his or her own words.

Ask your child to read the passage aloud. Then answer the questions together. When you finish, please sign below.

1. Why were more than 200 puppies used in *101 Dalmatians*? _____

_____

_____

2. How did the trainers teach the Dalmatian puppies? _____

_____

3. What happened to the Dalmatian puppies when the movie was finished?

_____

_____

4. What do Dalmatians look like? _____

_____

We completed this homework assignment together.

_____   _____
(child's signature)   (family member's signature)

Name _____

Date _____

230 Dalmatian Puppies

Did you know there is a movie about Dalmatian dogs? It is called *101 Dalmatians*, but 230 Dalmatian puppies and several grown Dalmatians were actually in the movie.

Why were so many puppies needed if the movie is called *101 Dalmatians*? It takes a long time to make a movie. *101 Dalmatians* was filmed in six months. The Dalmatian puppies grew quickly. Every two to four weeks, new puppies took the place of the older puppies. That way, the puppies would look like they were the same age all through the movie.

Trainers used food and fun to train the Dalmatian puppies. When the puppies did their scenes correctly, they got treats. They also got to play with toys and the trainers. This made the puppies want to do what the trainers asked them to do. If the puppies did what they were told, they got more food and fun. The puppies learned their parts quickly. They never refused to do a scene, and none of them had an "accident" on the set.

When the movie was finished, the last puppies were going to go back to their owners. The owners planned to find new homes for them. Instead, many members of the film crew took puppies home with them. One trainer took home four dogs!

If you get a chance to watch *101 Dalmatians*, see if you can spot all the different puppies.

Dalmatians are white dogs with black spots and mostly black ears. Their hair is very short.

Week-by-Week Homework: Reading Comprehension (Grade 3)
© Mary Rose, Scholastic Inc.

> **Standard:** Ask and answer questions to demonstrate understanding of a text, referring explicitly to the text as the basis for the answers.

Dear Family,

   The questions for this assignment are literal questions. This means that every answer is clearly stated in the passage. Your child can use words from the story, but do not allow him or her to copy whole sentences at this time.

   Remember that if your child makes an error when reading aloud, let him or her continue to read to the end of the sentence. It is very likely that he or she will hear the mistake and self-correct it. It is important for readers to listen to themselves as they read and know that what they are saying should make sense. This self-correction is a very valuable skill.

Ask your child to read the passage aloud. Then answer the questions together. When you finish, please sign below.

1. What country first made piñatas? _____

2. In what country did the piñata get its name? _____

3. What four steps happen before a child hits a piñata? _____

_____

_____

_____

_____

4. What is a "trick" piñata? _____

_____

_____

We completed this homework assignment together.

_____   _____
(child's signature)   (family member's signature)

Week-by-Week Homework: Reading Comprehension (Grade 3)
© Mary Rose, Scholastic Inc.

Name _____

Date _____

Piñatas

Everyone loves to break open a piñata [peen-YA-tuh]. Children often do this on Christmas or on a birthday. Here's how it's sometimes done. A piñata is decorated to look like an animal and then it's hung from a tree. The first child to take a turn is blindfolded. Then someone hands him or her a stick. The child is spun around in a circle, and everyone sings a song. Next, the child uses the stick to hit the piñata hanging above. If the child misses, the next person in line gets a chance to try. Everyone wants the piñata to break. It is the only way to get the candies hidden inside it.

Piñatas were first made long ago in China. Back then, they were shaped like a cow and used only at New Year's. The piñata was filled with different kinds of seeds. When the piñata was broken, the seeds fell out. Then the seeds were burned, and the ashes were kept for good luck.

Later, piñatas became popular in Europe. The name "piñata" comes from Italy. A "pignatta" [pe-NYA-tah] is a clay cooking pot, and that's what Italians used to make their piñatas. The Spanish also used a plain clay pot and then decorated it with ribbons and colored paper.

Then Spanish priests brought the piñata to North America. They found out that the Mayan and Aztec peoples of Mexico already had their own forms of piñatas.

At Christmas in Mexico, piñatas are filled with fruit and candies. Sometimes, people make a "trick" piñata. This piñata contains only flour, confetti, or water. The child who breaks this piñata is usually very surprised and unhappy. Often, someone will give him or her a basket of treats to make up for the disappointment.

Today, piñatas are made of paper because the clay pots are dangerous when they break. Many look like colorful animals or cartoon characters.

Week-by-Week Homework: Reading Comprehension (Grade 3)
© Mary Rose, Scholastic Inc.

Understanding main idea

Almost every reading assessment asks children to determine the main idea of a passage. A question may straightforwardly ask, "What is the main idea of the passage?" But questions about the main idea may also be phrased in the following ways: "What is this passage mostly about?" "What is the subject of this passage?" "What is the focus of this passage?" or "What is the topic of this passage?"

KEY IDEAS AND DETAILS

RI.3.2 Determine the main idea of a text; recount the key details and explain how they support the main idea.

Because the main idea of a passage can often be found in the title, a question may ask children to comment on the title or suggest an alternate title for a passage: "Why is 'Boomerang' a good title for this passage?" or "What would be another good title for this passage?"

All of these questions are basically asking children to determine the main idea of the passage. Guide children to recognize this type of question no matter how it's phrased.

Lesson about main idea

Try this main idea lesson with children: After the class has read a short informational article, like those found in Scholastic's *Storyworks* magazine (storyworks.scholastic.com), ask children to share the facts they remember from that article. Record responses on chart paper or on the chalkboard or whiteboard. List all responses as long they're actually from the article.

Next, read the list aloud and ask children to choose the three or four most important facts from the article. You might say, "When you get home tonight and tell your family that you read about boomerangs, what are the three most important facts you will tell everyone?"

As children determine the most important facts, circle or draw a star beside them. Talk about why they chose certain facts over others on the list. Guide children to see the difference between important ideas and the details that support them.

Finally, work with children to write a summary sentence that includes the three or four facts in a concise sentence. Repeat this lesson frequently during the school year. To help children master this skill, allow them to first practice it in small groups or in pairs before assigning it as an independent activity.

Please send this assignment back to school by _____ .
(date)

> **Standard:** Determine the main idea of a text; recount the key details and explain how they support the main idea.

Dear Family,

When your child writes a response to the questions below—or to similar questions on a test—it's important that he or she doesn't include his or her own background knowledge. The goal of the questions is to determine whether your child read and understood the passage, not to learn about his or her previous experiences. Your child's responses should be based solely on the information in the passage.

The main idea of a passage is often summed up in its title. That's why a question like the first one below asks the reader to supply an alternate title for the passage.

Ask your child to read the passage aloud. Then answer the questions together. When you finish, please sign below.

1. What would be another good title for this passage? _____
_____

2. Why does a boomerang return after you throw it? _____
_____
_____

3. What steps should you follow to throw a boomerang? _____
_____
_____
_____

4. In which country did people use boomerangs for hunting? _____

We completed this homework assignment together.

_____   _____
(child's signature)   (family member's signature)

Week-by-Week Homework: Reading Comprehension (Grade 3)
© Mary Rose, Scholastic Inc

Name _____ Date _____

Boomerangs

If ever you are alone and need something to do outside, try tossing a boomerang. When you throw a boomerang, it will come back to you.

Long ago, people in Australia used wooden boomerangs for hunting. Hunters threw boomerangs at animals to stop them. Today, people use boomerangs for fun. There are even contests to see who can throw a boomerang the farthest or hit a target with it.

A boomerang is shaped like your arm. The middle part of a boomerang is even called "the elbow." Like your elbow, it bends in the middle. This creates two "wings." These wings work just like airplane wings. As a boomerang flies through the air, its wings spin. Each wing turns toward the other wing. This makes the boomerang fly in a circle.

It isn't difficult to throw a boomerang, but it can be tricky to do it right. Hold the boomerang straight up and down. It should be close to your body, just above the shoulder. Now snap your wrist and throw! With practice, you can release the boomerang and make it come back to you in exactly the same spot. Try throwing a boomerang. It will seem like a friend is playing catch with you!

Week-by-Week Homework: Reading Comprehension (Grade 3)
© Mary Rose, Scholastic Inc.

Please send this assignment back to school by _____ .
(date)

> **Standard:** Determine the main idea of a text; recount the key details and explain how they support the main idea.

Dear Family,

The most often asked questions on state assessment tests are about finding the main idea of a passage. This may sound simple to us, but it is often difficult for children at this age. They often include supporting details rather than the most important ideas in the text.

One way to help your child determine the main idea of a text is to ask him or her to use only one sentence to recount what he or she read. The first question below asks your child to identify the main idea of "Animals Doing Tricks," and the rest of the questions are about details that support that main idea.

Ask your child to read the passage aloud. Then answer the questions together. When you finish, please sign below.

1. **Part A:** What is this article mostly about?

   a. A man who provides insects for movies   **b.** How spiders spin webs at night

   c. The movie *James and the Giant Peach*   **d.** How to train insects to do tricks

   Part B: Which detail from the article best supports your answer to Part A?

   a. "Kutcher takes very good care of his spiders and insects."

   b. "Some of his insects have appeared in movies like *Jurassic Park* and *James and the Giant Peach.*"

   c. "Kutcher put a tiny drop of honey on a fly's head."

   d. "He often gives talks to kids and adults about being nice to bugs."

2. How does Steve Kutcher get insects to perform for the camera? Give one example.

   _____

   _____

We completed this homework assignment together.

_____   _____
(child's signature)   (family member's signature)

Week-by-Week Homework: Reading Comprehension (Grade 3)
© Mary Rose, Scholastic Inc.

Name _____ Date _____

Animals Doing Tricks

You have probably seen dogs and lions and elephants doing tricks. You might have seen them in a circus or on TV. These animals are trained to do what the trainer says. Have you ever seen a movie that shows insects and spiders doing tricks? Of course, they cannot be trained to do what someone says, but these creatures do have a trainer.

One of these trainers is Steve Kutcher. Some of his insects have appeared in movies like *Jurassic Park* and *James and the Giant Peach.* Kutcher knows a lot about insects, but he has had to figure out how to get his insects to perform. In a scene in one movie, a spider was supposed to spin a web. Kutcher knew his spider would only spin at night, so that's when the scene was filmed.

In another movie, a fly was supposed to rub its head. Kutcher put a tiny drop of honey on a fly's head. The fly wanted to clean itself, so it rubbed its head and the director filmed it. Another time, the moviemaker wanted insects to come out of the stomach of a dummy, a doll that looks like a person. Kutcher put moths, worms, flies, and spiders inside a pipe. Next, he put the pipe inside the dummy's stomach. Then, Kutcher pushed the creatures out of the pipe.

Kutcher takes very good care of his spiders and insects. He often gives talks to kids and adults about being nice to bugs. He teaches about how insects help our world.

In the future, you may see a movie where bugs scare you or gross you out. Just remember that they may belong to Steve Kutcher. When you think about it, that's not really scary at all.

Week-by-Week Homework: Reading Comprehension (Grade 3)
© Mary Rose, Scholastic Inc.

Please send this assignment back to school by _____ .
(date)

> **Standard:** Determine the main idea of a text; recount the key details and explain how they support the main idea.

Dear Family,

The main idea of an informational article often appears in the first paragraph and is restated in the last paragraph. Sometimes, it can be found in the title of the article. After your child has read "Gabby's Gold" aloud to you, ask him or her to explain what this passage is mostly about. Then have your child use a crayon or pencil to find words or phrases in the passage that helped him or her identify the main idea.

Question 2 below has two parts. Although there is more than one correct answer for Part A, your child needs to justify the answer for only one response. Make sure his or her answer is from the text and not from any prior knowledge about Gabby Douglas.

Ask your child to read the passage aloud. Then answer the questions together. When you finish, please sign below.

1. What is the main idea of this article? _____

2. **Part A:** Circle the words that describe Gabby Douglas based on evidence from the text.

   a. successful   **b.** talented   **c.** lonely   **d.** short   **e.** strong

   Part B: Find a sentence in the passage that supports your response to Part A.

   _____

3. Why did Gabby's mother allow her to leave home at the age of 14? _____

   _____

4. What does the last sentence of the passage mean? _____

   _____

We completed this homework assignment together.

_____   _____
(child's signature)   (family member's signature)

Week-by-Week Homework: Reading Comprehension (Grade 3)
© Mary Rose, Scholastic Inc.

Name _____ Date _____

Gabby's Gold

by Ann Sullivan Sheldon

Gabrielle "Gabby" Douglas is the first African American gymnast to win an Olympic gold medal in the individual all-around event. In fact, during the 2012 Summer Olympics, she won two gold medals.

Gabrielle Douglas was born on December 31, 1995, in Virginia. She began training in gymnastics when she was six years old. She won a state championship when she was only eight. When she was 14, Gabby and her mother made a tough decision. They knew she needed to train with an Olympic coach. Gabby left her home and family to go to Iowa and train with Laing Chow. He had trained Shawn Johnson, who had become a world-champion gymnast and Olympic gold medalist. Maybe he could help Gabby win a gold medal, too.

Gabby moved in with the Partons, a family who lived in Iowa. They treated her as if she were a member of the family. Gabby's mother missed her daughter. However, she knew that Gabby was in a caring home.

In 2010, Gabby took part in the Junior National Championships and won her first medal. Soon, she was picked for the United States Olympic team. She was headed for the 2012 Summer Olympics in London, England.

Gabby became famous when her team won the gold medal in women's gymnastics. She also earned first place in the individual all-around event.

After the 2012 Olympics, Gabby spoke to groups and was on one of her favorite TV shows, *The Vampire Diaries*. She wants to go to college. First, though, she plans to compete in the 2016 Olympics. She hopes to win a third gold medal. It looks like "the sky is the limit" for Gabby!

Week-by-Week Homework: Reading Comprehension (Grade 3)
© Mary Rose, Scholastic Inc.

Connecting people, events, and ideas

This is a complex standard that requires children to identify and explain relationships between important aspects of a text, such as how one person's decision affected someone else, how a battle impacted a war, or how a scientific discovery led to a technological advance that changed the way we live. It helps to teach children about the different ways that these relationships can work. A few suggestions appear below.

KEY IDEAS AND DETAILS

RI.3.3 Describe the relationship between a series of historical events, scientific ideas or concepts, or steps in technical procedures in a text, using language that pertains to time, sequence, and cause/effect.

- A person can inspire, persuade, or pressure another person to take an action.
- A new invention can open new areas of study.
- An action can cause a reaction and set off a chain of events.
- A problem can prompt people to search for solutions.
- A process can require a specific sequence of steps to work.

Seeing how key people, events, and ideas are related is an important part of comprehension.

Integrated model of literacy

One of the main tenets of the Common Core State Standards is that they are an integrated model of literacy. This concept has definite implications for teachers in the elementary school. Although "integrated model" goes by many names (unit approach, thematic teaching, multidisciplinary integration, fusion, trans-disciplinary integration, project-based instruction) the concept is the same. The classroom is engulfed in a topic of study and all instruction centers on that subject. This is a wonderful way for children to make the kinds of connections that this standard requires.

For example, if your classroom is studying the voyage of Christopher Columbus, children could make the connection between this historic event and how it changed the world. They would use language that pertains to time and sequence, and they could study the reasons for (causes) and effects of his historic journey.

The first passage for this standard is about the Duryea brothers and how they revolutionized the design and selling of cars in the United States. The second passage explains how one of Edison's inventions spawned an idiom. The third passage explains how the discovery of a new type of dinosaur affected scientific ideas.

Please send this assignment back to school by _____ .
(date)

> **Standard:** Describe the relationship between a series of historical events, scientific ideas or concepts, or steps in technical procedures in a text, using language that pertains to time, sequence, and cause/effect.

Dear Family,

   This passage about the Duryea brothers is based on a historical event. It contains some words that will probably be unfamiliar to your child. Help him or her to understand that the names for things often change over time and that they often reflect technological changes in the products. For example, we first had a "talking machine," then a telephone, then a phone, and finally a cell phone, which we now often just call a "cell."

   Help your child see the importance of Duryeas' invention and how it affected our lives, even though their car company was not successful.

Ask your child to read the passage aloud. Then answer the questions together. When you finish, please sign below.

1. This passage contains four different words or phrases that mean "something people ride in to get from place to place." One of these is *car*. What are the other three?

   HINT: *They may not be familiar to you!* _____

   _____

2. How was Frank's car different from at least two others in the race?

   _____

3. What did the Duryea brothers do after the race? _____

   _____

4. How did the Duryea brothers make history? _____

   _____

   _____

We completed this homework assignment together.

_____
(child's signature)

_____
(family member's signature)

Week-by-Week Homework: Reading Comprehension (Grade 3)
© Mary Rose, Scholastic Inc.

The Duryea Brothers

You've probably seen shiny and colorful new cars for sale in car lots. Two brothers, Frank and Charles Duryea, started this idea over a hundred years ago.

On Thanksgiving of 1895, a small group of people in Chicago stood in the cold and snow. They were there to watch six cars set off on a 54-mile race. No one in the crowd had ever seen a car race before. Most of them, like other Americans, traveled by horse and carriage. Most had heard about the new "horseless vehicles" but had never seen one.

This race was for inventors to show off their cars. Eighty-nine men entered the race. Many of the cars broke down before they even got to Chicago. Only six drivers actually made it to the starting line. One of them, Frank Duryea, had been dreaming of this moment for years. In 1893, Frank and his brother Charles had created a gasoline-powered "motor wagon."

Frank Duryea in his prize-winning car

After a few miles of the race, two electric cars went dead. Another car ran into a ditch. Frank's car kept going. For a few minutes, his car went as fast as 10 miles an hour! This was much faster than traveling by horse. Nine hours later, Frank Duryea crossed the finish line. He won $2,000. The Duryea Brothers used this money to start a car company. It was the first company in the United States to make and sell more than one copy of the same type of car. The company didn't make money, but the Duryeas made something else. They made history!

Week-by-Week Homework: Reading Comprehension (Grade 3)
© Mary Rose, Scholastic Inc.

Please send this assignment back to school by _____ .
(date)

> **Standard:** Describe the relationship between a series of historical events, scientific ideas or concepts, or steps in technical procedures in a text, using language that pertains to time, sequence, and cause/effect.

Dear Family,

Help your child make a connection between the old phonograph and its lack of volume control to a modern situation you all may encounter, listening to the television or to music. For example, talk about how the buttons on a remote control can increase, decrease, or mute the volume of a television.

For Question 3, it is important to note that your child can correctly answer a question like this even if he or she is still not completely familiar with the technical language.

Ask your child to read the passage aloud. Then answer the questions together. When you finish, please sign below.

1. Who invented the first phonograph? _____

2. Instead of telling you to "put a sock in it," what might your parents say to you if your music is too loud? _____

   _____

3. The phonograph changed as inventors tried to make the sound better. What were the three ways they recorded sound? _____

   _____

   _____

   _____

   _____

We completed this homework assignment together.

_____   _____
(child's signature)   (family member's signature)

Week-by-Week Homework: Reading Comprehension (Grade 3)
© Mary Rose, Scholastic Inc.

Put a Sock in It!

Has anyone ever told you to "put a sock in it"? That might mean you are being too noisy. It might mean you are talking too much. The person wants you to be quiet. It is a funny thing to say. Where did we get this unusual phrase?

We know Thomas Edison invented the light bulb and many other things. He had one favorite invention. It was the phonograph, or "talking machine," which recorded sound and played it back. At first, the sound was very loud and scratchy. Other inventors made the phonograph better by changing from a tinfoil cylinder to a wax cylinder. Still others used a round disc that could spin. (We call these *records*!)

These musical machines were missing one important thing. There was no way to control the volume of sound they produced. There was no way to turn down the sound. The sound that came from the huge horn was very loud. People could not talk while the music played. The scratchy noise gave some people headaches.

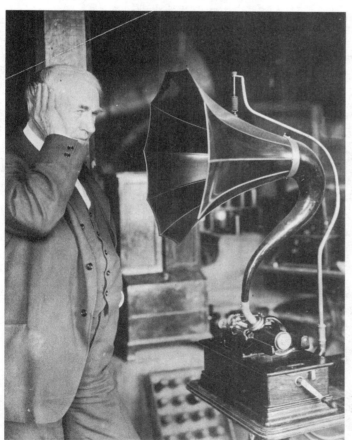

Thomas Edison listens to his invention.

To control the volume, people started stuffing socks into the horn to soften the sound. Up until the 1930s, teenagers were putting socks into their record players. It kept their parents from complaining about the loud music. Eventually, a sound control was invented. Then socks went back where they belonged—on people's feet. Today, though, if people tell you to "put a sock in it," you will know exactly what they mean. You will also know why they are using that funny expression.

Week-by-Week Homework: Reading Comprehension (Grade 3)
© Mary Rose, Scholastic Inc.

Please send this assignment back to school by _____ .
(date)

> **Standard:** Describe the relationship between a series of historical events, scientific ideas or concepts, or steps in technical procedures in a text, using language that pertains to time, sequence, and cause/effect.

Dear Family,

   This standard has several parts. This passage and questions focus on just one aspect: scientific ideas. Your child will determine why Spinosaurus took the crown of "king" of dinosaurs away from the T. rex and how scientists came to certain conclusions about the newly discovered Spinosaurus dinosaur. As you can see, both of these are scientific ideas. Although there are no questions about the time sequence here, your child may find it interesting to note that both the T. rex and the Spinosaurus were actually discovered at about the same time.

Ask your child to read the passage aloud. Then answer the questions together. When you finish, please sign below.

1. Why was T. rex known as the king of the dinosaurs? _____
   _____

2. Compare the Tyrannosaurus rex and the Spinosaurus. _____
   _____
   _____

3. Why do scientists think that the Spinosaurus stayed in the water most of
   the time? _____
   _____
   _____

4. What do scientists think that Spinosaurus ate? _____
   _____

We completed this homework assignment together.

_____   _____
(child's signature)   (family member's signature)

Week-by-Week Homework: Reading Comprehension (Grade 3)
© Mary Rose, Scholastic Inc.

Name _____ Date _____

The New King of the Dinosaurs?

Which was the biggest, meanest meat-eating dinosaur that ever lived? Most people would say it was the Tyrannosaurus rex. This dinosaur probably weighed about 9 tons, or 18,000 pounds, and was about 40 feet long. Fossils of the T. rex have helped scientists understand how big it was, how it moved, and what it ate. The first fossils from a Tyrannosaurus rex were found in 1892. For over a hundred years, most people believed that T. rex was the king of the dinosaurs.

Between 1910 and 1914, the fossils of another large dinosaur were found in Egypt in the Sahara Desert. It was called Spinosaurus [spy-no-SOHR-us]. The Spinosaurus fossils were destroyed during World War II. The building they were housed in was bombed. Scientists still had notes, drawings, and photographs of this dinosaur's  fossils, but they kept hoping to find more fossils of this dinosaur.

In 2009, a huge Spinosaurus fossil was found in the Sahara Desert, this time in Morocco. Scientists were now able to understand more about this dinosaur. The Spinosaurus was longer than the T. rex. It was heavier, too. Spinosaurus had six-foot-long spines down its back.

T. rex had very short front legs and walked on its back legs. Spinosaurus had long front legs and walked on all fours. Its short back legs had paddle-shaped claws. The Spinosaurus had a long snout like a crocodile's. These led scientists to believe that Spinosaurus spent most of its time in the water. They think it ate giant sharks and fish that were as big as cars.

What other secrets about dinosaurs are still buried in the earth? What will we learn about dinosaurs when other fossils are found?

Week-by-Week Homework: Reading Comprehension (Grade 3)
© Mary Rose, Scholastic Inc.

Affixes

In "Petoskey Stones," one of the passages for this standard, children will encounter the words *colony*, *polyp*, and *tentacles*. These are scientific words, specific for this domain. Many domains, especially science, use Greek and Latin affixes (prefixes and suffixes) with root words. The list of these is quite long, but this chart shows a few we use every day.

Appositives

Authors often use appositives to help readers understand an unfamiliar term or to explain something about a person or place. Appositives can be set off by commas or indicated by a dash. They can come at the beginning, middle, or end of a sentence; for example: *J. K. Rowling, author of the Harry Potter books, is the first person to make a billion dollars as an author.* (The appositive is after her name.) *The author of the Harry Potter books, J. K. Rowling, is the first person to make a billion dollars as an author.* (The appositive is placed at the start of the sentence.) *The first person to make a billion dollars as an author was J. K. Rowling, the author of the Harry Potter books.* (The appositive is at the end of the sentence.)

Teach children to look for and recognize appositives. Appositives are often the answer to test questions and, more important, they contain explanations for unfamiliar terms. My own students used to say, "They are a test question waiting to happen!" Margaret S. Gentile adds, "An appositive is a positive clue!" There are some appositives in the passage about Petoskey stones.

CRAFT AND STRUCTURE

RI.3.4 Determine the meaning of general academic and domain-specific words and phrases in a text relevant to a grade 3 topic or subject area.

PREFIX	MEANING	EXAMPLE
super-	more than	supermarket, superhuman
non-	not	nonfiction, nonstop
tri-	three	tricycle, triplets
multi-	many	multicolored, multipurpose
sub-	under	submarine, subtropic
tele-	at a distance	telephone, telegraph
auto-	self	automobile, autobiography
photo-	light	photosynthesis, photograph
SUFFIX	**MEANING**	**EXAMPLE**
-able	able to	fixable, doable
-er, -or	one who	baker, professor
-ful	full of	careful, helpful
-fy	make	beautify, simplify
-ly	like, in the manner of	carelessly, fearlessly
-some	having that quality	lonesome, fearsome

Please send this assignment back to school by _____ .
(date)

> **Standard:** Determine the meaning of general academic and domain-specific words and phrases in a text relevant to a grade 3 topic or subject area.

Dear Family,

As children reach the upper elementary grades, they will begin to read more and more domain-specific text. This means that they will be exposed to words that are relevant for specific subject areas, such as science, math, and social studies. This article about the Petoskey stone includes domain-specific words related to science.

The passage contains two appositives—one for **coral colony** and one for **hexagon**. Help your child see that this is how the author provides a definition for an unfamiliar term. Appositives can often help children answer test questions, so remind your child to look for appositives as he or she reads about Petoskey stones.

Ask your child to read the passage aloud. Then answer the questions together. When you finish, please sign below.

1. What is a Petoskey stone? _____

_____

2. What was the job of the tentacles on a polyp? _____

_____

_____

3. How many sides does a polyp have? _____

4. What is the dark spot in the center of each polyp? _____

_____

We completed this homework assignment together.

_____   _____
(child's signature)   (family member's signature)

Week-by-Week Homework: Reading Comprehension (Grade 3)
© Mary Rose, Scholastic Inc.

Name _____   Date _____

Petoskey Stones

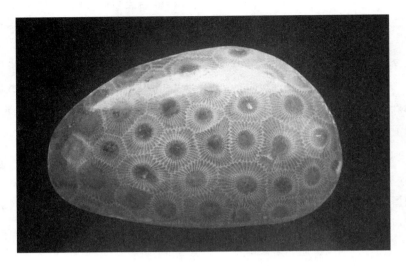

If you study a rock, you can often tell how it was formed. Sometimes you can tell where it came from. Some rocks have stripes. They may have been at the bottom of an ocean or lake. Some rocks are black and shiny and smooth. They may have come from a volcano. What if a rock has polka dots?

This is a picture of a Petoskey stone [pa-TOS-kee]. It was found on the beach at Lake Michigan. This Petoskey stone is not just old. It was made about 350 million years ago. That's before there were dinosaurs!

Very long ago, the area we now know as Michigan was at the bottom of a sea. In this place, tiny corals lived together in a group, a **coral colony.** When you look at a Petoskey stone, you are looking at a coral colony. Each coral is called a *polyp*. Each polyp has six sides, which is a **hexagon**. The dark dot in the center of each hexagon was the mouth of the coral. The mouth had tiny tentacles around it. The tentacles pulled food into the coral's mouth.

After the coral colony died, it lay at the bottom of the sea for millions of years. The coral colony became a fossil. This means that it turned from an animal into stone.

It is hard to find Petoskey stones on a Michigan beach. When the stones are dry, you cannot see the markings. But if you spray them with water, the pretty coral polyps appear. When people do find a Petoskey stone, they often polish the stone to make the corals easier to see. Petoskey stones are so pretty that people usually set them on a shelf and admire them.

Week-by-Week Homework: Reading Comprehension (Grade 3)
© Mary Rose, Scholastic Inc.

> **Standard:** Determine the meaning of general academic and domain-specific words and phrases in a text relevant to a grade 3 topic or subject area.

Dear Family,

The questions on this assignment are all literal questions. This means that the answers are directly stated in the passage. The focus is on fruits and vegetables and how scientists decide which is which. This domain is science in general, botany in particular. Please help your child understand any words that are unfamiliar to him or her.

Part A of question 2 has only one correct answer and it must be supported by a sentence in Part B. Help your child read the sentences in Part B carefully to decide which one helped him or her determine the meaning of "savory."

Ask your child to read the passage aloud. Then answer the questions together. When you finish, please sign below.

1. How do scientists decide whether a food is a fruit or a vegetable? _____

_____

2. Part A: What is the meaning of the word *savory*? Circle the word.

a. sweet   **b.** hot   **c.** juicy   **d.** salty

Part B: Circle the sentence from the passage best helps the reader understand the meaning of *savory*.

a. "A tomato is really a fruit, like apples and grapes."

b. "All five of these fruits are called 'vegetables' because they are savory."

c. "Instead of being sweet, a tomato is a little salty or tangy."

d. "They are not eaten for dessert after a meal; they are part of the main meal."

3. Besides the tomato, what other foods that we call vegetables are really fruits?

_____

We completed this homework assignment together.

_____   _____
(child's signature)   (family member's signature)

Tomatoes

What do all of these foods in the box have in common?

vegetable soup, salsa, chili, pizza, baked beans, ketchup

If you guessed "tomatoes," then you are correct! All of the foods on this list contain tomatoes. Usually, the tomatoes are crushed and cooked so that we can't even see them. We can taste them, though, and their special flavor helps us enjoy foods. But are tomatoes fruits or vegetables?

The study of plants is called *botany*. Scientists who study plants are called *botanists*. They can tell whether a plant is a fruit or vegetable by how it grows and makes seeds. A tomato is really a fruit, like apples and grapes. It is actually a berry! The tomato is often called a vegetable because it is savory. Instead of being sweet, a tomato is a little salty or tangy. It tastes like a vegetable, not a fruit. Other savory "vegetables" are green beans, eggplants, squash, cucumbers—but wait! All of these foods are a lot like the tomato! According to botanists, they are fruits, too!

All five of these fruits are called "vegetables" because they are savory. They are not eaten for dessert after a meal; they are part of the main meal. They are full of vitamins and minerals that help you grow strong and stay healthy.

In 2014, the heaviest tomato weighed 8 pounds and 6.5 ounces. A massive tomato tree growing inside Walt Disney World's Epcot may be the largest single tomato plant in the world. This plant has a harvest of more than 32,000 golf ball-sized tomatoes each year. They are served at Walt Disney World restaurants.

Tonight, if someone tells you to eat your vegetables, you can reply that you would rather eat fruit instead—and then dive into some salsa!

Week-by-Week Homework: Reading Comprehension (Grade 3)
© Mary Rose, Scholastic Inc.

Text features

Generally speaking, nonfiction is more difficult for most children to read and understand than fiction. Young readers can be overwhelmed by the volume of information they encounter on a page of informational text: the deck (the brief descriptor underneath the title), sidebars, pronunciation guides, subheads, maps, graphs, charts, and captions. Children sometimes skip text features when they're reading for information, but important facts are often placed and clarified in text features. They often summarize or visually represent information, both of which make the article easier to understand.

CRAFT AND STRUCTURE

RI.3.5 Use text features and search tools (e.g., key words, sidebars, hyperlinks) to locate information relevant to a given topic efficiently.

The passages for this standard contain several text features. "Shooting Stars" has photos and captions. The pelican narrator in "Pelican Pete" shares facts, but the labeled photograph on the page identifies the parts of a pelican's body mentioned in the text. "Lady Liberty" features a sidebar with a fun fact and offers two web links that will give more information about the famous statue.

Lesson idea for teaching text features

This is a gradual-release lesson. Start with the whole group and then gradually release responsibility for practice to small groups, and then assign it as independent work. It can be done with paper, in computer labs, or on tablets.

Take children on a scavenger hunt to help them understand text features. Select a particularly "busy" article from magazines such as *Ranger Rick*, *Scholastic News*, *National Geographic Kids*, or a section from a science or social studies textbook. Create a list of questions in which answers can be found only in the article's text features—the deck, a caption, map, graph, or chart. Leave space for children to write their answers and tell where they located the information in the article.

Conduct the first lesson as a whole-group activity. Ask a volunteer to share the answer to the first question. Pause to allow every child to locate the information. Identify the text feature that contains the answer. If children need additional time to complete the answer to the question, give them a minute or two to do so. Repeat this process for each question. It may take about 45 minutes to complete ten questions.

The second time you do this activity, begin by reviewing the names of the different kinds of text features. Then ask children to answer the questions with a partner or in a small group.

By the third time, children should be able to answer the questions independently. If they enjoy this text feature scavenger hunt, choose several passages and have children work in teams to create their own list of questions for their classmates. Collect the questions and redistribute them for different teams to answer.

Please send this assignment back to school by _____ .
(date)

Standard: Use text features and search tools (e.g., key words, sidebars, hyperlinks) to locate information relevant to a given topic efficiently.

Dear Family,

This standard requires your child to identify key words and to use text features, such as sidebars and illustrations, to get more information about the topic of the passage. The key words in "Shooting Stars" appear in *italics* to help your child locate them and understand the importance of these words. A pronunciation guide follows the words that may be unfamiliar so your child will know how to say them. In the guide, the syllable to be stressed is capitalized, so your child will know to say that part of the word with more emphasis.

The photographs with the passage show a shooting star and a comet. The additional information will help your children see the difference between the two.

Ask your child to read the passage aloud. Then answer these questions together. When you finish, sign below.

1. How is a meteoroid different from a meteorite? _____

_____

_____

2. What is a meteor? _____

_____

3. What causes a meteoroid to light up? _____

_____

4. What causes meteor showers? _____

_____

We completed this homework assignment together.

_____   _____
(child's signature)   (family member's signature)

Week-by-Week Homework: Reading Comprehension (Grade 3)
© Mary Rose, Scholastic Inc.

Shooting Stars

Have you ever seen a streak of white light across a night sky? You may have called this a "falling star" or a "shooting star." What you saw was not a star at all. It was actually a *meteoroid* [MEE-tee-ur-oyd]. A meteoroid is a piece of dust or rock from space. When a meteoroid gets close to Earth, the air causes it to burn up. When you see a shooting star, it is really a meteoroid on fire. The streak of light it makes is called a *meteor* [MEE-tee-ur].

Look at the arrow to find a shooting star.

Sometimes, a meteoroid does not burn up completely. It lands on Earth. This is called a *meteorite* [MEE-tee-ur-ite]. If a meteorite hits Earth very hard, it causes a *crater*. A crater is a hole in the earth.

We can see meteors all the time. Sometimes there are lots of them at once. This event is called a *meteor shower*. When Earth passes through the tail of a *comet*, it passes through lots of pieces of dust and rock. On those nights, you can see lots of meteors. The best times to see a meteor shower are from late July to mid-August and from mid-October to mid-December.

Keep looking up at the night sky. You might see a shooting star on any night!

A comet is made up of ice, rock, and gases. It is sometimes called a "dirty snowball."

Please send this assignment back to school by _____ .
(date)

> **Standard:** Use text features and search tools (e.g., key words, sidebars, hyperlinks) to locate information relevant to a given topic efficiently.

Dear Family,

Text features contribute more information to the main body of an informational text. These features include maps, charts and graphs, sidebars, pronunciation guides, hyperlinks to websites, and captions.

This assignment focuses on the text feature known as an annotated illustration. This passage is written in the first person, so it reads as if a pelican is sharing the information. The labels in the photograph identify some of the parts of a brown pelican's body that the narrator describes in the text. Make sure your child uses information from both the text and the annotated illustration to answer the questions below.

Ask your child to read the passage aloud. Then answer the questions together. When you finish, please sign below.

1. What parts of the pelican's body make it easier to swim? _____

_____

2. What is the name for the pouch that is part of the pelican's bill? _____

_____

3. What makes it possible for a pelican to fly? _____

4. Which words does the author use for the bird's mouth?

HINT: *Look at the photo, too.* _____

_____

5. Name two ways that a pelican uses its body to get food. _____

_____

We completed this homework assignment together.

_____   _____
(child's signature)   (family member's signature)

Week-by-Week Homework: Reading Comprehension (Grade 3)
© Mary Rose, Scholastic Inc.

Name _____ Date _____

Pelican Pete

by Ann Sullivan Sheldon

There is nothing better than a day at the beach! I love flying over the deep blue sea. I'm always hungry for a fish or two. You may have seen me as I soar through the sky. My wingspan—the measurement of my wings from tip to tip—is over 6 feet! My sharp eyes help me find prey from far away. Then I dive into the water and scoop up my meal in my fishing basket. Well, it's actually my bill, but it stretches out like a basket or pouch for catching fish. I can hold up to 3 gallons of water in my pouch. The water drains out and leaves the fish behind. I have a hook at the top of my mouth that helps me hold onto those wiggly fish. Fishermen don't want me around because I catch more fish than they do!

When I am not fishing, I swim well. My webbed feet and strong, short legs are a great help. I breathe through my mouth. I'm 8 years old, which is old for a brown pelican like me. I weigh only about 10 pounds. That is because my bones are full of air pockets. The air makes me light so that I can fly. The next time you see me overhead, I may be with my friends. We always fly together in a V or a straight line. We'll probably be heading for an island near the shore.

Upper mandible

Lower mandible

Gular pouch

Week-by-Week Homework: Reading Comprehension (Grade 3)
© Mary Rose, Scholastic Inc.

Please send this assignment back to school by _____ .
(date)

> **Standard:** Use text features and search tools (e.g., key words, sidebars, hyperlinks) to locate information relevant to a given topic efficiently.

Dear Family,

Authors often use print conventions such as asterisks (*), **boldface print,** or *italics* to help readers find information quickly. They use text features such as subheads to separate information into categories and to clarify unfamiliar terms. This article also has a sidebar, a box that contains additional information about a topic. Your child can also find the answers to number-related questions by quickly scanning the article for dates, numerals and word names for numbers, and units of measure, such as **feet** and **pounds**.

Ask your child to read the passage aloud. Then answer the questions together. When you finish, please sign below.

1. In what section of the passage did you read about the spikes on Lady Liberty's head?

_____

2. How long did it take to assemble the 350 pieces of the statue? _____

3. Why has the Statue of Liberty turned green? _____

_____

4. Where did you find the explanation to answer question 3? _____

5. Why is there a broken chain at Lady Liberty's feet? _____

_____

6. How could you find information about visiting the crown? _____

_____

We completed this homework assignment together.

_____   _____
(child's signature)   (family member's signature)

Name _____   Date _____

Lady Liberty

by Ann Sullivan Sheldon

The Statue of Liberty, also called Lady Liberty, stands in New York Harbor. This symbol of freedom was a gift from the people of France in 1885. America was just over 100 years old then. The Statue of Liberty was packed in crates and shipped on a boat from France to New York. There were over 350 pieces. It took four months to put the statue together!

Torch At night, hundreds of light bulbs light the Statue of Liberty's torch. The torch is said to guide the way for immigrants. They are people coming from another country to seek freedom in America. In 1986, for the statue's 200th birthday, the torch was rebuilt and covered in thin sheets of gold.

Crown There are seven spikes in Lady Liberty's crown. Each spike is nine feet long and weighs about 150 pounds. The spikes stand for the world's seven oceans and seven continents. Visitors can climb 377 steps inside the statue to peek out of one of the 25 windows in the crown. To find out more about how to visit the Statue of Liberty's crown, go to http://www.nps.gov/stli/planyourvisit/visit-the-crown.htm.

Tablet The Statue of Liberty holds a tablet with the date JULY IV MDCCLXXVI. These Roman numerals mean July 4, 1776. This is the date that America became a new country.

Base The statue stands on a pedestal, or base, that is 154 feet high. From the bottom of this base to the tip of her torch, the statue is 305 feet tall. A broken chain stands at the feet of Lady Liberty. Because the chain is broken, it stands for freedom. To learn about visiting the base, go to http://www.nps.gov/stli/planyourvisit/visiting-the-pedestal.htm.

> ### Fun Fact
> Lady Liberty is made of copper. Over the years, air and water have weathered the statue and caused it to turn from bright orange copper to green. This process is called **oxidation.**

Point of view

The Common Core State Standards recognize that not only is it important to have opinions, but it is also important to be able to state those opinions logically, defend them with facts, and separate personal views from the points of view of authors.

CRAFT AND STRUCTURE

RI.3.6 Distinguish their own point of view from that of the author of a text.

The passage "The Big Cheese" is likely to spark some interest and curiosity in your classroom. Children may be surprised to learn the actual size of the piece of cheese that was delivered to President Jefferson as a gift. Use a yardstick or tape measure to demonstrate the size of the cheese. You might also tell your class that 1,600 pounds is about the weight of a small car. These facts may help children determine whether they agree with the man who thought such a big cheese would make a great gift for the president.

Similarly, children may agree or disagree with the author of "Bull Riders and Rodeo Clowns," who believes that rodeo clowns should be as famous as bull riders. What is important in thinking about this passage is not whether readers agree or disagree, but that they are able to find support for their arguments in the passage. Unlike classroom discussions in which children can expound on their personal experiences, on standardized tests, young readers can only use the information contained in a reading passage to justify their position.

Self-correction

When families ask for suggestions about how to help their child grow as a reader, be sure to explain the importance of self-correction. When they (or you) are listening to a child read aloud and hear a mistake, it's important to resist the temptation to immediately correct the error. Allow the child to read to the end of the sentence, and even into the next one. The reader will usually pause because he or she realizes something is wrong. Most children instinctively go back and reread to correct a mistake. If the reader cannot correct the error, wait a moment or two to allow him or her to think through the problem. A child should not need more than ten seconds (count them!) to figure out a new word. If the child cannot make sense of the word or phrase, then you can give a hint, or just say the word.

The ability to listen to oneself read is a huge part of reading for meaning and comprehension. If we immediately and automatically correct an error, the child will never develop the habit of paying close attention to every word. If we deny children this opportunity to make sense of the unfamiliar, we will handicap them in future reading assignments when the work is more difficult or no guidance is available.

Week-by-Week Homework: Reading Comprehension (Grade 3)
© Mary Rose, Scholastic Inc.

Please send this assignment back to school by _____ .
(date)

> **Standard:** Distinguish their own point of view from that of the author of a text.

Dear Family,

   This standard asks your child to distinguish his or her own point of view from that of the author of a text. The passage "The Big Cheese" is about an unusual gift. Does your child agree or disagree that this unusual gift was a good idea? Make sure he or she can use information in the text to explain his or her position. Point out that the sidebar contains information about a gift of cheese to another president.

Ask your child to read the passage aloud. Then answer the questions together. When you finish, please sign below.

1. Why did Mr. Leland want to send a gift to President Jefferson? _____
_____

2. Why did Mr. Leland think cheese would be a good gift? _____
_____

3. Explain whether President Jefferson's cheese was a good gift. Use details from the passage to support your answer. _____
_____
_____

4. Explain whether President Jackson's cheese was a good gift. Use details from the passage to support your answer. _____
_____
_____

We completed this homework assignment together.

_____
(child's signature)

_____
(family member's signature)

Week-by-Week Homework: Reading Comprehension (Grade 3)
© Mary Rose, Scholastic Inc.

Name _____ Date _____

The Big Cheese

Have you ever thought about sending a gift to the President of the United States? What would it be? Would you send a drawing you made yourself? Information about the history of your town? Would you send a piece of cheese to the president?

In 1801, many Americans loved President Thomas Jefferson. Our third president was an American hero. He wrote the Declaration of Independence.

He doubled the size of the United States. He was charming and smart. Because of these reasons, a man named John Leland, from Cheshire, Massachusetts, decided to send President Jefferson a present: a piece of cheese.

Leland didn't want to send a slice of cheese that would fit on a sandwich. He wanted to send the biggest cheese anyone had ever seen. Leland asked everyone who loved President Jefferson to donate a day's worth of milk so it could be made into cheese.

The people of Cheshire, Massachusetts, loved the idea. They mixed all the milk curds and pressed it in a large cider press. When the cheese dried, it weighed 1,235 pounds. It was wider than four feet and thicker than one foot.

John Leland traveled for three weeks to take the cheese to Washington, D.C. President Jefferson displayed the cheese in the White House for several years!

Another Big Cheese

President Andrew Jackson also received a gift of cheese. It weighed 1,400 pounds. This cheese, however, was very stinky. Jackson had to get rid of it because it was smelling up the White House. He invited everyone to come and eat it. About 10,000 people showed up. Within two hours, the cheese was gone. It took a little longer for the smell to leave, though.

Week-by-Week Homework: Reading Comprehension (Grade 3)
© Mary Rose, Scholastic Inc.

Please send this assignment back to school by _____ .
(date)

> **Standard:** Distinguish their own point of view from that of the author of a text.

Dear Family,

   After your child reads aloud this passage about bull riders and rodeo clowns, talk about whether he or she agrees or disagrees with the writer's opinion, which is stated in the final paragraph. It is important for your child to form an opinion based on the information in the passage and to be able to go back to the text to find details that support that opinion. It is also important for your child to realize that his or her views may differ from the author's text. At this point, it does not matter if they agree or disagree; it matters that they can justify their stand.

Ask your child to read the passage aloud. Then answer the questions together. When you finish, please sign below.

1. How long does a rider have to stay on a bull to win points? _____

2. What kinds of special clothing does a bull rider wear? _____

_____

3. The writer thinks rodeo clowns should be as famous as the bull riders.

Do you agree? Circle one: **YES**   **NO**

4. Using details from the text, tell why you agree or disagree with the writer.

HINT: *Find at least two ideas to support your idea.* _____

_____

_____

_____

We completed this homework assignment together.

_____   _____
(child's signature)   (family member's signature)

Bull Riders and Rodeo Clowns

The angry bull storms out of the gate, kicking his back legs in the air. He is trying to buck the bull rider off his back. The rider holds a rope with only one hand. His other hand is waving in the air, and it cannot touch the bull. He wears leather gloves and cowboy boots. He wears chaps over his jeans. He wears a cowboy hat or a helmet.

The bull bucks again, rears, kicks, spins, and twists. The bull rider is trying to stay on the bull for eight seconds. This has been called "the most dangerous eight seconds in sport." If the rider stays on for that long, he earns points. If he gets thrown off, then the bull gets the points. More people are hurt riding bulls than in any other rodeo sport.

Most riders are hurt after the ride is over. When the rider tries to get off, he can get tangled in the rope. He can be whirled around or stomped by the bull. If the rider does get off safely, he is still in danger. The bull might charge and aim his sharp horns at the rider.

That's when the rodeo clowns step in. They do make the crowd laugh, but their main job is to make sure riders don't get hurt. They wear clown faces and brightly colored, baggy costumes. They act funny and tease the announcers. That changes when a bull and rider are let loose. That's when their real job begins. If the rider gets tangled in the rope, one clown might jump around crazily to get the bull's attention. Then another clown can free the rider from the rope. If the rider is on the ground or running to climb a fence, the clowns will scream, run in front of the bull, or wave hats. They do anything they can to keep the bull away from the rider.

At the rodeo, it is usually the bull riders who get all of the attention. When the announcers say their names, the crowd cheers. Rodeo clowns deserve as much or more fame and attention. Their lives are in danger, too. They are in danger all evening long, not just for eight seconds.

Week-by-Week Homework: Reading Comprehension (Grade 3)
© Mary Rose, Scholastic Inc.

Accessing text features

We want children to be able to access and digest information from illustrations, maps, photographs, charts, and other kinds of text features in print and digital media. The first passage for this standard explores the relationship between clownfish and sea anemones. The photograph shows just how close this relationship is and are annotated with information that builds on the facts in the main body of the text. The second passage, "Hop, Leap, Run!," is a poem about games that have been played for hundreds of years. Children have to guess which game is described in each stanza. The accompanying photos and caption give them additional clues.

INTEGRATION OF KNOWLEDGE AND IDEAS

RI.3.7 Use information gained from illustrations (e.g., maps, photographs) and the words in a text to demonstrate understanding of the text (e.g., where, when, why, and how key events occur).

Lesson idea for teaching text features

Try this lesson to teach children the value of text features: Allow each child to choose a different animal to study. Provide clear guidelines about what you want them to learn about their animal (e.g., habitat, predators or prey, physical characteristics, and/or interesting ways this animal has found to survive in the world). As children locate print and/or digital information, have them write notes— a few sentences from each of their information sources.

For the report, give each child a sheet of 12 x 18 white drawing paper and ask them to create a poster that contains the information in their notes. Have them include several text features. For instance, they might use subheads to identify topics, drawings and captions, and/or maps. A sidebar might tell about the physical characteristics of the animal. Most children will enjoy creating a colorful presentation, and this format allows struggling readers to show their artistic skills. *Note:* If children use colored pencils rather than crayons or markers, the poster will be much neater; crayons tend to smear, and markers can soak through and bleed on the paper.

Allow children to do research at home, but insist they make their poster during class time. Ask them to present their posters to the class before you hang the work in a classroom display. As an alternative, choose famous people in history to study or common objects.

Please send this assignment back to school by _____ .
(date)

> **Standard:** Use information gained from illustrations (e.g., maps, photographs) and the words in a text to demonstrate understanding of the text (e.g., where, when, why, and how key events occur).

Dear Family,

   Authors and editors include text features such as maps, charts, captions, illustrations, and sidebars in informational texts to help readers understand the topic. Text features include information that enhances the main body of a text. Help your child answer the questions below by looking not only at the text but also at the text feature—the information in the photograph.

Ask your child to read the passage aloud. Then answer the questions together. When you finish, please sign below.

1. About how long is a clownfish? _____

2. How does the clownfish help the sea anemone? _____

_____

_____

3. How does the sea anemone help the clownfish? _____

_____

_____

4. Why do most fish stay away from anemones? _____

_____

_____

5. How does the clownfish protect itself from the anemone? _____

_____

_____

We completed this homework assignment together.

_____   _____
(child's signature)   (family member's signature)

Week-by-Week Homework: Reading Comprehension (Grade 3)
© Mary Rose, Scholastic Inc.

Name _____ Date _____

Clownfish and Sea Anemones Together

Many of you know Nemo, the little clownfish in the movie *Finding Nemo*. Nemo is an imaginary fish. A real live clownfish is about 11 centimeters long. That is about 4 inches, which is about as long as your hand.

Nemo was orange and white, but clownfish can also be purple or red or yellow. They all have white lines that look like the paint on a clown's face. That is why they are called "clownfish." There are 28 kinds of clownfish in all.

Clownfish live inside sea anemones (uh-NEM-uh-nees), which are ocean animals that look like flowers. Inside an anemone, a clownfish is safe from bigger fish. But the clownfish also helps the anemone by keeping it clean. It also chases away the anemone's enemies, like the butterfly fish.

This living arrangement is a good one for both species. Clownfish live in an anemone for their whole life. Both animals work together to help each other.

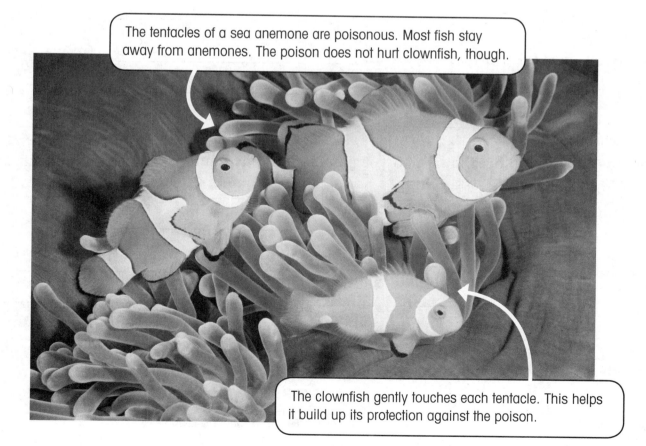

The tentacles of a sea anemone are poisonous. Most fish stay away from anemones. The poison does not hurt clownfish, though.

The clownfish gently touches each tentacle. This helps it build up its protection against the poison.

Week-by-Week Homework: Reading Comprehension (Grade 3)
© Mary Rose, Scholastic Inc.

Please send this assignment back to school by _____ .
(date)

> **Standard:** Use information gained from illustrations (e.g., maps, photographs) and the words in a text to demonstrate understanding of the text (e.g., where, when, why, and how key events occur).

Dear Family,

Make sure to remind your child to study the photographs to help them identify each game described in the poem. You may also want to review what a stanza is. A stanza is a group of lines in a poem; it's like a paragraph. Stanzas are separated by a space. This poem contains four stanzas.

For extra fun, go outside and play these games. Playing them may bring back some of your childhood memories! Talk about why you and your child think these games are still being played.

Ask your child to read the passage aloud. Then answer the questions together. When you finish, please sign below.

1. List the games in the poem. _____

_____

2. What does the word *scotch* mean? _____

_____

_____

3. Tell how a photograph helped you understand one game. _____

_____

_____

4. How long have children been playing these games? _____

_____

We completed this homework assignment together.

_____   _____
(child's signature)   (family member's signature)

Week-by-Week Homework: Reading Comprehension (Grade 3)
© Mary Rose, Scholastic Inc.

Name _____ Date _____

This poem is about games children have been playing for about 1,000 years.
Can you guess the names of these games? Have you ever played them?

Hop, Leap, Run!

Do you like to hop, hop,
On the chalk-drawn scotch,
And skip over the box that
Holds your rock?

A "scotch" is a line drawn on the ground.

Over your friend's back
You leap like a frog
And crouch in front for others
To pretend you're a log.

If I touch you, you're it—
An age-old game—
Back and forth—gotcha!
For centuries the same.

Hiding in the bushes,
Quiet as can be,
As the seeker comes a-peeking,
Seeking all my friends—and me.

Week-by-Week Homework: Reading Comprehension (Grade 3)
© Mary Rose, Scholastic Inc.

Finding connections in writing

Children who are still learning to read often benefit from reading nonfiction articles that have a clear structure. These texts will have an introduction that clearly states the main idea, two to four paragraphs in the body to support it, and a conclusion that sums up or restates the main idea. In the passages for this standard, the opening and closing are "written in a circle." This means that there is a connection between the introductory and the closing paragraphs. Often, the text will contain one or two elaborations in the form of examples or definitions. We want children to learn by reading and writing these simple structures, but we also want them to advance to more sophisticated and imaginative ways of expressing facts and details. For example, more advanced articles may first elaborate on the topic, but the actual topic sentence might be located in the middle or the end of the introductory paragraph.

INTEGRATION OF KNOWLEDGE AND IDEAS

RI.3.8 Describe the logical connection between particular sentences and paragraphs in a text (e.g., comparison, cause/effect, first/second/third in a sequence).

Each topic sentence in the passages for this standard is italicized. The main points the authors make to support the topic are underlined. In the passage "Do Your Shoes Talk?," children can make connections between cause and effect and comparisons between the two types of shoes the writer describes. "Jumbo" shows the connection between the current use of a word and its origin. Children can also identify the sequence of events in Jumbo the elephant's life.

Recognizing clue words

When making comparisons, authors often use key words such as *alike, similarly, both,* or *also*. When making contrasts, they may use words such as *however, whereas, instead, unlike,* or *on the contrary*. Teaching children to identify these key words in a text will help them see the logical comparison-contrast connections in it.

Similarly, when identifying cause and effect, guide children to look for signal words such as *since, consequently, as a result of,* or *because*. Typically these words signal that an explanation of the cause or the effect is about to follow. Readers should look for a cause or an effect before and after these clue words.

Please send this assignment back to school by _____ .
(date)

> **Standard:** Describe the logical connection between particular sentences and paragraphs in a text (e.g., comparison, cause/effect, first/second/third in a sequence).

Dear Family,

We want children to realize that the thesis statement of many (not all!) informational texts is in the opening paragraph. In this passage, the thesis sentence appears in *italics*. The main points, called topic sentences, the author is making about the thesis, are <u>underlined</u> in each paragraph. These should help your child see the connection between the main idea and the points that support it. The questions below guide your child to compare and contrast and identify a cause-and-effect relationship.

Of course, our shoes do not really "talk," but they do say a lot about us. If necessary, help your child understand what the author means when she writes that shoes can talk.

Ask your child to read the passage aloud. Then answer the questions together. When you finish, please sign below.

1. When you read the first sentence, what did you think the passage would be about?

_____

2. What might be true about a person who wore crakows with very short toes?

_____

3. Tell one way that chopines and crakows were alike. _____

_____

4. Tell one way that chopines and crakows were different. _____

_____

5. Why did women wearing chopines need help? _____

_____

We completed this homework assignment together.

_____   _____
(child's signature)   (family member's signature)

Name _____   Date _____

Do Your Shoes Talk?

by Ann Sullivan Sheldon

JEUNE ÉLÉGANT EN 1480
(Dingels Jungemun.)
XVᵉ SIÈCLE

Throughout history, one could usually learn something about a person just by looking at his or her shoes. Today, if you wear cowboy boots, flip-flops, ballet slippers, or hockey skates, people can guess what you enjoy doing. In a way, your shoes talk about you!

In the past, some people did not have any shoes at all, and others had to pay dearly for them. In ancient Greece, slaves were not allowed to wear shoes. In England in the 1700s, a workingman's shoes cost him half of all the money he made in a month.

A man's shoes also said whether or not he was important. In 14th-century Europe, wealthy men wore shoes called "crakows." These shoes had pointed toes with a long curled tip. Sometimes the toes of crakows had to be stuffed with moss or hay to keep the tip pointy. Laws about these shoes were strict. A king could wear shoes with toes as long as he liked. Noblemen could have shoes whose toes were 24 inches long. Gentlemen could have crakows with toes that were 12 inches long. Lowly commoners could have only 6-inch toes on their shoes.

In those days, rich women often wore fancier shoes than poor women. In Venice in the 16th century, women wore shoes called "chopines." The soles of these shoes were very tall. At first, the soles were eight inches high, but rich women wanted them even higher. Soon, the soles of chopines for the richest women were up to 30 inches high! Of course, women wearing chopines could not walk in them. The women had to have servants hold onto their elbows as they moved!

Today, we can still learn about people by looking at their shoes. What do your shoes say about you?

Week-by-Week Homework: Reading Comprehension (Grade 3)
© Mary Rose, Scholastic Inc.

Please send this assignment back to school by _____ .
(date)

> **Standard:** Describe the logical connection between particular sentences and paragraphs in a text (e.g., comparison, cause/effect, first/second/third in a sequence).

Dear Family,

The thesis sentence of this passage appears in *italics*. The sentences that are <u>underlined</u> are topic sentences that support the thesis sentence. These are the sentences that contain answers to the questions below.

Young readers need to identify the connections between the parts of an informational text like this one. Pay careful attention to question 1, as it asks about that connection.

Ask your child to read the passage aloud. Then answer the questions together. When you finish, please sign below.

1. Circle the sentence from the passage that tells you the connection between the elephant and the word *jumbo*.

   a. "In America, Jumbo traveled in a private railroad car painted red and gold."

   b. "In the late 1880s, one of the most famous creatures in the world was an elephant."

   c. "Believe it or not, when we talk about something that is really big, it's because of an elephant."

   d. "That is more than 12,000 pounds!"

2. Name all the places, in order, where Jumbo lived. _____
   _____

3. Name three things that we might label as "jumbo." _____
   _____
   _____

We completed this homework assignment together.

_____   _____
(child's signature)   (family member's signature)

Week-by-Week Homework: Reading Comprehension (Grade 3)
© Mary Rose, Scholastic Inc.

Jumbo

Have you ever seen the Jumbotron at a basketball game? Have you ever ordered a jumbo pizza or drink? Have ever seen a jumbo jet? Has someone in your family ever bought a jumbo box of laundry soap or a jumbo package of paper towels? *Why do we call things "jumbo"?*

Believe it or not, when we talk about something that is really big, it's because of an elephant. In the late 1880s, one of the most famous creatures in the world was an elephant. This was no ordinary elephant. He weighed over six tons! That is more than 12,000 pounds! He was 11 feet tall from his feet to his shoulders. The elephant was named "Jumbo."

Jumbo was captured in the jungles of Africa and shipped to Europe. Then, he was sold to a zoo in Paris, France. Later, Jumbo lived in England in the London Zoological Gardens. Finally, he came to America after being purchased by circus owner P. T. Barnum. In America, Jumbo traveled in a private railroad car painted red and gold. He was so famous his picture was in newspapers and magazines. Jumbo's picture was also on the labels of thread, baking powder, and toothpaste. Soon, everything that was very large was called "jumbo."

As you can see from the list above, the word *jumbo* is no longer used to refer to an elephant. Today, it actually means "something really huge." Think about this the next time you read about a "jumbo" anything!

Week-by-Week Homework: Reading Comprehension (Grade 3)
© Mary Rose, Scholastic Inc.

Evaluating sources of information

Today, children need to be adept at gleaning and synthesizing information from print and digital sources: textbooks, other books, newspapers and magazines, websites, and blogs. Try to supplement every unit of study with a variety of information sources. Help children determine whether information is relevant and credible. Learning how to evaluate information will help children become better readers and more critical thinkers.

INTEGRATION OF KNOWLEDGE AND IDEAS

RI.3.9 Compare and contrast the most important points and key details presented in two texts on the same topic.

Paired text and types of questions

The passages for this standard are paired texts. Almost every state-developed assessment, as well as the Partnership for Assessment of Readiness for College and Careers (PARCC) and Smarter Balanced Assessment Consortium (SBAC), use paired texts on their assessments. Depending upon whether a text is literary or informational, children will analyze paired texts for the following reasons:

1. To compare literary elements
2. To compare central ideas, topics of the same event/point of view
3. To compare different versions of the same text
4. To analyze how ideas are transformed from one text to another
5. To integrate information from passages for a purpose
6. To compare structures
7. To analyze supplemental elements

These assessments also have these kinds of questions about paired texts:

A. Questions about points of view
B. Questions about the focus and quality of evidence
C. Questions about differences in emphasis
D. Questions about omission and/or inclusion of ideas between two texts
E. Questions about changes from an original to a derivative text
F. Questions about the synthesis of ideas to fully understand the topic

The paired texts for this standard ask children to compare central ideas, which, in this case, are the habits of a leopard. The first passage is an informational article and the second passage is a poem, but both contain similar facts.

Please send this assignment back to school by _____ .
(date)

> **Standard:** Compare and contrast the most important points and key details presented in two texts on the same topic.

Dear Family,

   In these paired passages, the article presents facts about leopards in prose, while the poem relays almost the same information. To answer the questions below, your child compares both passages to see which information appears in only one passage and which appears in both.

Ask your child to read the passages aloud. Then answer the questions together. When you finish, please sign below.

1. Name one fact you learned from the article, "Can You Spot the Leopard?"

_____

2. Name one fact you learned from the poem, "The Leopard." _____

_____

3. What information about the leopard is the same in each passage? _____

_____

4. **Part A:** What is the meaning of the word *adaptable* in "Can You Spot the Leopard"?

   a. able to see at night   **b.** able to hide easily
   c. able to climb trees   **d.** able to live in different places

   Part B: Which sentence helps you understand this meaning?

   a. "They can live anywhere, from desert to tropical rainforests."

   b. "They hunt at night and spend most of the day resting or draped over a tree limb."

   c. "No two leopards have the same markings."

   d. "Adult leopards can be about six feet long and can weigh between 100 and 150 pounds."

We completed this homework assignment together.

_____   _____
(child's signature)   (family member's signature)

Week-by-Week Homework: Reading Comprehension (Grade 3)
© Mary Rose, Scholastic Inc.

Can You Spot the Leopard?

by Ann Sullivan Sheldon

It's nighttime in the jungle, and all seems peaceful. Don't be fooled! Under cover of darkness, a deadly game of hide-and-seek is being played out. The hiders are animals that feed on plants. The seekers are **predators**. Predators hunt and kill other animals for food. One of the most feared predators is the leopard.

The leopard is a big cat. Adult leopards can be about six feet long and can weigh between 100 and 150 pounds. The leopard's coat is sandy-colored with black spots. These black spots are good camouflage. They make it easy for the leopard to hide in the shadows without being seen. These black spots are called "rosettes." They are like human fingerprints. No two leopards have the same markings.

Leopards are **nocturnal**. They hunt at night and spend most of the day resting or draped over a tree limb. Leopards are stealthy, cunning, and adaptable. They can live anywhere, from deserts to tropical rainforests. Few animals are a match for the fast, fierce, and powerful leopard.

The Leopard

Anonymous

The leopard creeps quietly
Creeps in the night
Creeps when the stars
And the moon are bright.

The leopard creeps powerfully
Looking for its prey
Waiting to pounce by night
Then he sleeps all day.

The leopard creeps softly
Up on the hill
Peeps from the bushes
Waiting to kill.

Answers

Literary Texts

Super Hound, p. 16
1. writing a book report 2. a cartoon dog who asks Leo to help him solve a problem 3. He goes with Super Hound to try to find the missing money. 4. his finished book report on "Jefferson's Challenges"

The Ferris Wheel, p. 18
1. 1904 World's Fair in St. Louis 2. *excited;* she talks and waves to her mother 3. Accept any: Tommy's stomach does a flip. He holds onto the bar. He doesn't look down. He closes his eyes. He doesn't wave to Mama from the top. He has to pry his hands off the bar. 4. Tommy doesn't want Mama and Julia to know he was afraid.

Jewels and Toads: A French Folktale, p. 21
1. She doesn't love Emma as much as she loves her other daughter. "She made Emma work hard and walk a mile to the well to get fresh water." 2. Emma was nice to the woman. Mila was mean to her. 3. Sample response: Be kind to everyone. 4. "Once upon a time"; "lived happily ever after."

Anansi, the Firefly, and the Tiger: An African Folktale Retold, p. 24
1A. b, e 1B. Accept any of the following for b (sneaky): "He always played tricks on other animals and then laughed at their bad luck." "Anansi decided to trick Tiger and eat all the leftover eggs." Accept any of the following for e (greedy): "'This one is for me!' He dropped the egg into his basket." "He thought they were his anyway, so he should not have to share."
2. The moral is that if you are greedy, you might get nothing. This is what happened to Anansi. He wouldn't share with anyone, and he ended up with nothing.
3. He'd been pinched by the lobster and didn't want the others to know he was trying to sneak in and eat the eggs.

The Dragon and the Stone, p. 27
1. a 2. d 3. c

The Elephant's Child, p. 30
1. the Elephant's Child 2. Act 1 3. to tell part of the story, including the setting 4. The crocodile wanted to eat the Elephant's Child.
5A. d 5B. "He asked ever so many questions."

What Is the Best Fruit?, p. 33
1. "Apples" 2. grapes 3. Answers will vary, but children should cite details in the poem as support.

The Trojan Horse, p. 36
1. 40 2. The Trojans thought the statue was a parting gift from the Greeks because they had won the war. 3. First the Greeks built a wooden horse. Some soldiers hid inside. Then the other Greeks pretended to leave. When the horse was inside the city of Troy, the rest of the Greek army sailed back. The soldiers climbed out of the horse and were joined by the rest of the army. 4. Don't trust an enemy who suddenly becomes nice.

The Council of Mice / The Lion and the Mouse, p. 39
1. a mouse 2. It's not enough to have a great idea; you must be willing to carry it out. 3. The lion doesn't eat the mouse when he could. 4. The mouse chews the ropes that trapped the lion. 5. Even the smallest creature can be a big friend; one good turn deserves another.

The Sword in the Stone / The Lady of the Lake, p. 42
1. Arthur, Merlin, Sir Kay 2. Accept any reasonable answer that can be justified with details from the text. 3. In "The Sword in the Stone," Arthur becomes king when he gets the sword. In "The Lady of the Lake," he is already king. 4. Merlin is a sorcerer and a tutor to King Arthur.

Informational Texts

230 Dalmatian Puppies, p. 46
1. The movie took six months to make, and the puppies grew fast. 2. Trainers used food and fun. They gave the puppies treats and played with the puppies. 3. Some of the people from the movie took puppies home. Owners also found new homes for them. 4. Short hair, white with black spots and mostly black ears

Piñatas, p. 48
1. China 2. Italy 3. The child is blindfolded, gets a stick, spins in a circle, and everyone sings a song. 4. A piñata that contains only flour, confetti, or water and no treats

Boomerangs, p. 51
1. Answers will vary but should refer to the main idea of the passage—A boomerang is a toy that returns to the thrower. 2. The straight parts of the boomerang are like wings on an airplane, and they make it spin in a circle. 3. Hold the boomerang straight up and down, close to your body just above the shoulder. Snap your wrist and throw it. 4. Australia

Animals Doing Tricks, p. 53
1A. a 1B. b 2. Examples: Steve knew that the spider would spin a web at night, so the movie was filmed at night. Steve knew the fly would rub its head if he put honey on its head.

Gabby's Gold, p. 55
1. Gabby Douglas worked hard to win an Olympic gold medal in gymnastics. 2A. a, b, e 2B. Answers will vary. 3. Gabby needed to train with a well-known coach in Iowa. 4. There is nothing Gabby cannot achieve if she continues to work hard.

The Duryea Brothers, p. 58
1. horse and carriage, horseless vehicles, motor wagon 2. Frank's car used gasoline. 3. They started a car company. 4. They won the first car race in America. They were also the first to make and sell more than one copy of the same type of car.

Put a Sock in It!, p. 60
1. Thomas Edison 2. They might say to turn it down, use earphones, or use ear buds. 2. a tinfoil cylinder, a wax cylinder, and a round disc that could spin

The New King of the Dinosaurs?, p. 62
1. T. rex was believed to be the biggest, meanest meat-eating dinosaur. 2. Same: large dinosaurs; Different: T. rex lived on land and walked on two feet. Spinosaurus lived mostly in water and ate fish and walked on all four legs. Spinosaurus was longer and heavier. 3. Spinosaurus had paddle-shaped claws and a long snout like a crocodile's. 4. giant sharks and fish

Petoskey Stones, p. 65
1. A Petoskey stone is a coral colony that died millions of years ago and turned into a fossil. 2. Tentacles pull food into the coral's mouth. 3. 6 sides 4. the mouth of the coral

Week-by-Week Homework: Reading Comprehension (Grade 3)
© Mary Rose, Scholastic Inc.

Tomatoes, p. 67
1. Scientists look at the way a plant grows and makes seeds. 2A. d 2B. c 3. green beans, cucumbers, squash, eggplants

Shooting Stars, p. 70
1. A meteoroid is a piece of dust or rock in space; a meteorite has landed on Earth. 2. A meteor is the streak of light made when a meteoroid burns up. 3. The air around the earth causes the meteoroid to catch on fire. 4. A meteor shower happens when Earth passes through the tail of a comet.

Pelican Pete, p. 72
1. short, strong legs and webbed feet 2. gular pouch 3. wings and lightweight bones 4. mandible, beak, fishing basket, bill 5. Accept any two: sharp eyes to spot fish; pouch to scoop fish; hook to hold onto fish

Lady Liberty, p. 74
1. "Crown" 2. four months 3. oxidation or a chemical reaction between air and water and metal 4. the "Fun Fact" sidebar 5. The broken chain stands for freedom. 6. Go to the web link at the end of the text in "Crown."

The Big Cheese, p. 77
1. He thought Jefferson was a good man and a good president. 2. He wanted to send a special kind of cheese that was a gift from the people and from his town. 3. Answers will vary but should include details from the text in support. 4. Answers will vary but should include details from the text in support.

Bull Riders and Rodeo Clowns, p. 79
1. 8 seconds 2. leather gloves, cowboy hat or helmet, jeans, boots, chaps 3. Answers will vary. 4. Agree: Clowns help protect bull riders; they are in danger all evening long; they help entertain the crowd. Disagree: Clowns are not really in much danger; they do not ride the bulls and will not be thrown to the ground or stomped on; all they do is run around and act silly all evening long.

Clownfish and Sea Anemones Together, p. 82
1. about 11 centimeters (4 inches) 2. Clownfish keep sea anemones clean and scare away other fish. 3. Sea anemones protect clownfish by letting them hide and live in their tentacles. 4. The anemone's tentacles are poisonous. 5. The clownfish gently touches each tentacle to build up protection against the poison.

Hop, Leap, Run!, p. 84
1. hopscotch, leapfrog, tag, hide-and-seek 2. a line drawn on ground 3. Answers will vary. Sample responses: I never played hopscotch, but the picture helped me see how it is played. I did not know what leap frog meant until I saw kids leaping over each other's backs in the photo. 4. about 1,000 years

Do Your Shoes Talk?, p. 87
1. Responses should mention the history of shoes and how they give information about the people wearing them. 2. He probably wasn't very rich or important. 3. Both told about the person's importance or wealth. 4. The crakows were long and pointy; the chopines had very high soles. A commoner could own crakows, but not chopines. 5. The shoes were so high, women needed someone to help them walk.

Jumbo, p. 89
1. c 2. Africa, France, England, America 3. Accept answers from the text or children's own experiences.

Can You Spot the Leopard? / The Leopard, p. 92
1. Accept any fact in "Can You Spot the Leopard?" 2. Accept any fact in "The Leopard." 3. The leopard only hunts at night and rests during the day. 4A. d 4B. a

Week-by-Week Homework: Reading Comprehension (Grade 3)
© Mary Rose, Scholastic Inc.

Yearly Assignment Grid

PASSAGE/STANDARD	NOTES AND COMMENTS